Introduction

When your get-up-and-go has gotten up and gone, it's time to stop and recharge before you head back out at breakneck speed. That's what a coffee break is for, and that's what *Coffee Break Devotions—Latte* is about—to take a moment out of your hectic day to ponder the deeper things of life. If we are to be the very best that we can be, it is vital to take time out to replenish and refocus, to gain perspective and to consider more fruitful ways of living.

With coffee in all kinds of flavors and blends, coffee breaks have never been more pleasurable. So kick back with a cup of your favorite brew, done up just the way you like it, and enjoy these upbeat meditations just the size of a coffee break. Afterward, energized and refreshed, you can head back out on the road and *really* set your world in motion!

There can be no faith so feeble that
Christ does not respond to it.

No Waiting

When we've made a telephone call, many of us have had to punch our way through a maze of unfathomable pathways, only to be put on hold while listening to an inane repeating message. What if it were like this to reach God?

We might hear something like this:

Thank you for calling Heaven. Listen carefully—our options have changed:

Press 1 for requests.

Press 2 for thanks.

Press 3 for questions of faith.

For all other matters, press 4.

Next you might hear:

I am sorry, but God is busy helping other people. Your call is important to us, so please stay on the line. Your call will be answered in the order it was received. Estimated wait time: two hours and twenty minutes.

Most of us would hang up in utter frustration, but those facing a crisis *might* hang on. Thankfully, we don't have to endure telephone bureaucracy in order to reach God. Yet some of us approach God as if we do. The truth is, God is ready to hear you—anytime, anyplace, regardless of the frame of mind you happen to be in. Talk to Him. It's easier than picking up the phone and much less aggravating.

~

God is ready to take your call.
No waiting required.

Before they call I will answer; while they are still speaking I will hear.

Isaiah 65:24

I am satisfied that when the Almighty wants
me to do or not to do any particular thing,
he finds a way of letting me know it.

You Don't Need
a Burning Bush

A young man agonized over which college to attend. He sent letters to various universities and was accepted by several. One of the schools was the Colorado School of Mines—an in-state school with the benefits of residence-rate tuition.

His favorite aunt stopped by for a visit and asked him if he had made a decision about which school to attend. Looking pained, he replied that he had prayed about it and was waiting for a sign from God.

His wise aunt suggested they list the schools of choice across the top of a piece of paper, then

8

list under each tuition costs, proximity to family, rating of program, and scholarships awarded. The School of Mines was the clear leader. The aunt suggested that what they saw on the paper before them might be the sign from God. "Why not accept what seems to be the best option," she said. "If it's not meant to be, you will have a growing uneasiness, and God will let you know."

Volumes have been written about discerning the will of God. History tells us that God works through many avenues—our desires, circumstances, intuition, and counsel from wise people—sometimes all at once. Approach situations with prayer, then stay alert for what God will show you.

When all the signs point in one direction,
don't look for a burning bush.

Does not wisdom call out? . . .
Counsel and sound judgment are mine;
I have understanding and power.

PROVERBS 8:1, 14

No man is an island, entire of itself;
every man is a piece of the continent,
a part of the main.

Get Connected

There's a little mountain town with a grocery store, some quaint shops and restaurants, and not much else. You can be sure that if you're a local and you visit one of these places a few times, the shop owners or servers will know your face and, most likely, your name. Although people live spread out around the town, there is a central place for them to go for a sense of community.

With the tendency people have in our present age to move from place to place, it's increasingly difficult to connect, to establish ourselves within our towns. Even when houses are close, people tend to drive into their garages at the end of the day and hunker down inside their homes. Yet it's no less important for us to try to build a sense of community where we live.

If you feel this sense of connectedness lacking in your life, make a habit of frequenting the same places for a few weeks. Favor the smaller venues. Make having coffee at the local café part of your weekly routine. Get to know the people who live and work around you. In a society that's growing more and more impersonal, it takes greater effort; but we can connect with our communities. No man is an island—enjoy the people God brings into your life!

Don't be a stranger in
your own hometown.

They devoted themselves . . . to the fellowship,
to the breaking of bread and to prayer.

Acts 2:42

To know one life has breathed easier
because you have lived . . .
this is the meaning of success.

Be an Energizer

People who talk to Alison Smithe feel good afterwards, even if they've asked a question to which she's had to say no. It is likely that if Alison were in the middle of a crisis in her personal life, she'd still take time to listen to other people talk about their troubles and send them on their way feeling better. She's effervescent—always smiling, full of life—and she speaks with enthusiasm. If you were to share with her even the simplest accomplishment or blessing you have received, she'd reply, "Good job! That's great," and she'd mean it sincerely.

The key to Alison's success isn't that she's cheerful by nature—though that is a positive quality. The key is that Allison is genuinely interested in people, whether it's someone's baby's diaper rash or that someone close to you has died. When people talk to her, she asks thoughtful questions. She's an energizer. People leave conversations with her feeling charged.

Christ admonished His followers to put others' interests before their own. Listening to and celebrating others with enthusiasm doesn't necessarily come easily to all of us. Yet when we can allow God's love to flow through us and show a genuine, unselfish interest in others, we not only energize them, we get a charge out of it too.

~

It doesn't take super-human energy
to be an energizer—just some
true interest and compassion.

*Each of you should look not only
to your own interests, but
also to the interests of others.*

PHILIPPIANS 2:4

13

We pardon as long as we love.

Give Me a Break

Erica sat alone at a table in a quaint little restaurant on a Wednesday afternoon. Every so often, she'd look toward the door. She read the menu and reviewed her date book. Finally, she used her cell phone to call her friend, who was supposed to have met her there thirty minutes earlier. She left her friend a message, saying that she was waiting for her at the restaurant, hoped her friend was OK, and thought that she must have forgotten about their lunch date.

Erica had several choices. She could have become annoyed, sitting there alone wondering, but she didn't. She very well could have left a nasty message for her "irresponsible" friend, but she didn't do that either. Last, she could have stomped out of the restaurant in a huff. Instead, she ordered herself a nice salad, picked up the local edition paper, and enjoyed her lunch.

Erica's friend called that night, falling all over herself with apologies. She thought their lunch had been scheduled for the following Wednesday. The friend was relieved, and they both looked forward to their lunch the following week.

In this world of ultra-busy schedules, it's easy to forget things now and then. The next time someone inconveniences you, choose to believe the best of the individual. Give others a break—you never know when you might need one yourself!

Take the high road —
give others a break.

Bear with each other and forgive whatever
grievances you may have against one another.
Forgive as the Lord forgave you.

COLOSSIANS 3:13

Self-control is the ability to keep cool
while someone is making it hot for you.

Graduation Day

Rose grew up with a mother whose explosive temper sent everyone—including the pets—running for cover. Sadly, when Rose reached adulthood, she repeated the pattern, which seemed beyond her control. Her family and friends tiptoed around her to avoid saying anything to set her off, making all of her relationships strained.

At the suggestion of a brave friend, Rose began to see a counselor. Together they began to identify patterns in her thinking and behavior. After time, she could not only identify the patterns, but she worked to stop them. It was a tough process, looking at herself so closely. Her counselor advised Rose to add prayer to her routine. Anytime she felt the hot molten tendencies rising, she prayed. It seemed to help.

Then came a true test. A friend, upset with Rose, lashed out at her—yelling, shaking her finger, trying to provoke her. *So this is what it feels like,* Rose said to herself. She turned to her friend and said in a quiet tone, "I am sorry you are so angry with me. If you'd like to discuss the matter when you can do so calmly, I'll be available," and she turned away. Later, her friend apologized. When her counselor learned of the incident, she was elated. "Rose," she said, "I think you're ready to graduate."

~

It takes hard work to change, but through Christ, change is possible.

A gentle answer turns away wrath.

PROVERBS 15:1

By compassion we make others' misery our own,
and, by relieving them, we relieve ourselves.

Been There and Done That

Joan had always been an upbeat go-getter who really had her act together. Her friend Anne seemed to be just the opposite. Anne experienced divorce and lost her mother to cancer all in the span of a year. It had been several months, but Anne couldn't seem to get her usual spunk back. She found it hard to cope with the simplest things in life, cried often, and lost the will to climb out of bed in the morning. Anne was, by all indications, terribly depressed. Joan tried to be sympathetic, but in private she told her husband that Anne simply needed to pull herself up by the bootstraps and get on with life.

About the time that Anne finally began to recover, Joan suffered a great loss—and then another. While she tried to pull herself out of the muck and mire, she couldn't seem to reclaim her old self. The sadness felt like someone had socked her in the stomach, and the pain wouldn't go away. Compassionate toward her plight, Anne shared how counseling helped her get over the grief she had suffered and suggested that Joan might do the same.

Joan was surprised at the ironic turn of events but took solace in the fact that if Anne could overcome her grief, she could too.

~

Experience is often the best teacher of compassion and understanding.

Be completely humble and gentle;
be patient, bearing with one another in love.

EPHESIANS 4:2

I thank thee, O Lord. Thou hast set
eternity within my heart that no earthly
thing can ever satisfy me wholly.

Eternal Rewards

Thomas à Kempis was a monk at the beginning of the fifteenth century; and although his external life was simple, his inner, spiritual life was rich with devotion to God. People today still benefit from his insights. What many believe to be his crowning achievement was his editing of a diary by Gerhard Groote. Kempis' version became a book called *Imitation of Christ,* which many believe has had a profound impact on the body of Christ.

In contrast, shallow externals beckon us to turn away from the quiet waters within. We are constantly bombarded with images touted as the ideal, from what car one should drive to the size and shape of one's body. Keeping up with the Jones' can

20

become a never-ending rat race if we fall for its deceptive allure.

Although nothing is wrong with looking one's best or driving a fancy sports car, these externals will not follow a person into eternity, nor will they satisfy the spiritual hunger within. On the contrary, developing one's relationship with God and seeking first His righteousness will bear fruit in this age and ages to come.

On a daily basis we are given opportunities to choose society's values, which are here today and gone tomorrow, or to invest in inner riches and heavenly rewards. Why not seek God first today!

Developing your inner life is an
investment in your eternal future.

"Do not store up for yourselves treasures on earth, where moth and rust destroy, and where thieves break in and steal. But store up for yourselves treasures in heaven."

MATTHEW 6:19-20

Don't judge a tree by its bark.

Appearances Can Be Deceiving

Ruth, a marketing coordinator recently turned stay-at-home mom, attended a baby shower. Being more confident in the boardroom than in the world of diapers and baby formula, she was struggling with the adjustment and felt out of her element. The fact that she only knew the mother-to-be and overheard the women happily swapping updates on their children only added to her feeling of awkwardness.

A chipper woman took the seat next to Ruth. *These women sure look happy. I bet being a mother comes easily to them,* thought Ruth, assuming this woman and the others to be veteran mothers and homemakers.

The woman introduced herself as Linda, and shortly they were chatting about their children and their lives in general. Before long, it was obvious that she and Linda had far more in common than she had previously thought. As it turned out, Linda and most of the women in the group also had thriving careers prior to becoming stay-at-home moms.

"I felt like a duck out of water after my first child was born," offered Linda.

Soon it was apparent that God had brought a new friend into Ruth's life who not only could relate to her feelings, but also shared some spiritual insights that had helped her navigate through the transition into motherhood.

~

Don't judge a book by its
cover without reading
a few chapters first.

Judge not according to the appearance.
JOHN 7:24 KJV

Cold words freeze people, and hot words
scorch them, and bitter words make them bitter,
and wrathful words make them wrathful.
Kind words also produce their image
on men's souls; and a beautiful image it is.
They smooth, and quiet, and comfort the hearer.

Telling the Truth

Vickie was frank and very funny. She met people easily, and no one was a stranger. On the other hand, she had a hard time developing deep and long-standing relationships.

In sharp contrast was the one friend with whom Vickie had a history. Anne and Vickie had been neighbors growing up and had shared many classes together throughout their school years. Anne was not nearly as gregarious as Vickie, but she had much more meaningful, enduring friendships, something Vickie envied. Loneliness and spending weekends and holidays virtually alone motivated Vickie to begin analyzing her predicament.

What is it about Anne that everyone seems to love so much? I'm the one with the more dynamic personality?

Vickie began comparing how she and Anne had handled similar situations, especially conflicts. Whereas Vickie was quick to state her opinion and "call a spade a spade," Anne generally waited to be asked for her opinion. And when in a situation where the truth could hurt, Anne had a way of cushioning the truth with love and affirmation. Proverbs 12:18 confirmed her assessment: "Reckless words pierce like a sword, but the tongue of the wise brings healing."

Once she saw the light, Vickie was determined to become a healer and put her hurtful ways behind her.

∼

Speak the truth as you'd want to receive it.

Let your conversation be always full of grace, seasoned with salt.

COLOSSIANS 4:6

25

The road to a friend's house is never long.

True Hospitality

Chances are, most of us can remember a house where the kids liked to hang out when we were growing up. It probably wasn't a squeaky-clean house with vinyl on the furniture. Most likely it was a house with stacks of laundry, some scattered books and papers, and some dust. There may have been children's artwork on the fridge, and Kool-Aid was probably involved. Homes like these are warm places where kids feel safe, accepted, and free to have some fun.

With this in mind, why do we think things have to be just so before we will allow others into our inner sanctum? Could it be our own pride or insecurity?

Warmth and openness are two qualities that set others at ease and make them feel welcome. Most people find these attributes in short supply as they go about their everyday lives. It is unlikely that guests will feel compelled to give your furniture the white-glove treatment, yet offering genuine hospitality is a gift your guests will long remember and appreciate.

So why not turn a blind eye to those dust bunnies and invite a friend over today? Chances are, you'll be glad you did.

Don't let the specter of dust
keep you from opening
your home to friends.

Offer hospitality to one another.

1 PETER 4:9

Angels listen for your songs,
for your voice rises to the very
gates of heaven when you praise Me.

Praise in the Darkness

In Revelation 4, we read a glorious description of God having the appearance of jasper and carnelian. A rainbow encircles His throne, and He is surrounded by living creatures who cry out continually, "Holy, holy, holy is the Lord God Almighty, who was, and is, and is to come." He is so glorious, even the rocks cry out praise to Him!

It is easy for us to imagine praising God around His throne, but what about during the difficult times here on Earth? The apostle Paul and his companion Silas were imprisoned for their faith, yet in their darkest hour they sang praises to God. It was their way of saying, "Regardless of our circumstances, Lord, we praise You. We know You are at work." It was an expression of their faith, and it set the supernatural into motion. While they were singing, an earthquake erupted so violently that it shook the prison doors open and all the prisoners' chains were loosed.

Are you in the midst of your own dark hour? Take comfort in the fact that you are not alone. God is at work for you even when things look darkest. Begin lifting your voice in praise to Him, and see what miracles He works for you.

In the midst of darkness,
light a candle of praise.

Praise him for his surpassing greatness.

PSALM 150:2

There is in life no blessing like affection;
it soothes, it hallows, elevates, subdues, and
bringeth down to earth its native heaven:
life has nought else that may supply its place.

The Miracle of Touch

A couple traveled overseas to adopt a baby. When they met her for the first time, they saw a tiny child who looked much younger than fourteen months old. At that age most babies toddle around. This little girl could barely support the weight of her head, let alone her body. Nevertheless, the couple took her home and spent lots of time holding her close and talking to her. They had loved this child for months before they held her, and they were more than ready to express it.

The couple started the little girl on a more nutritious diet, and soon she could sit up on her own. When the family returned to visit the adoption agency, the workers who had met the child just eight weeks earlier couldn't believe it. And she was not simply satisfied with walking; when her feet hit the ground, she insisted on running, with the support of her dad's hands holding hers above her head.

Babies need and respond to affection; and it's imperative to healthy development. Let's not forget that we adults need it too. Is there someone in your life who could use a hug today? It's healthy emotionally and even physiologically, and it will make you feel good too.

A simple hug can work wonders.

[Jesus] took the children in his arms,
put his hands on them and blessed them.

MARK 10:16

27

Of all nature's gifts to the human race,
what is sweeter to a man than his children?

Through the Eyes of a Child

Donna Olafski, a concerned looking first-grader, cornered her friend Kelly on the playground.

"I know who the tooth fairy is," Donna said, after losing her first tooth the day before.

"Who?" asked Kelly earnestly. Donna related the story of seeing her own father enter her room and slip a dollar bill under her pillow.

After school Kelly went directly to her mother and blurted out, "Mom, I know who the tooth fairy is."

Her mom said, "Really? Who is it?"

She replied, "It's Mr. Olafski."

One can imagine the conversation and laughs that ensued

between Kelly's parents and the Olafskis, who themselves were good friends.

Children have a take on the world that can range from profound to hilarious. What a joy it is to listen to them, to see life through their eyes, and to remember what it was like to be in their shoes. It's easy for us to get bogged down by a multitude of responsibilities, yet God has provided refreshing entertainment for us in our children.

Who needs the television when children provide a steady stream of material better than any sitcom! Getting down on a child's level provides him or her with needed attention, and it's a great way to enjoy the gift God has given you.

Tap into the wonder of childhood
with the little ones in your life.

Children are a gift from the LORD;
they are a reward from him.

PSALM 127:3 NLT

Anyone who builds a relationship on less than openness and honesty is building on sand.

A Better Strategy

Faith thought she was being the bigger person. When Frank, her husband of six months, did things that bothered her, she didn't say much. Although she was inwardly irritated over certain incidents, she didn't feel they were worth mentioning. Isn't that what Christians are supposed to do? Frank had no idea he had been pushing Faith's buttons.

Then one day it happened. There was a small incident concerning groceries, and Faith blew a gasket. She not only reamed Frank for the grocery debacle, she reached back and began to sling all the incidents from the past six months at him. He was stunned.

Appalled at her own behavior, Faith was ashamed that she had erupted in such a destructive manner. After a meek and sincere apology, she and Frank set about to develop a more proactive way of dealing with issues. First they discussed in a non-threatening manner the sources of irritation. After all, they were still getting to know one another, and Frank had been pushing buttons without realizing it. They then vowed that as issues arose, they would take the time to resolve them instead of letting them build up.

What could have developed into a destructive pattern had been intercepted and turned into a loving and healthy strategy for a successful marriage.

"Who would have thought the explosion was one of the best things that could have happened to us?" Frank whispered in her ear on their first anniversary.

~

Deactivate issues before they can explode.

Let all bitterness . . . be put away from you.
EPHESIANS 4:31 KJV

Nor can a man with grace his soul inspire,
More than the candles set themselves on fire.

The Remedy

Jenny had become a big ball of uptight nerves. Her senior paper was due in a few days, yet the harder she tried, the less creative she became. Rather than take a break, she became more determined with each passing hour to press through and conquer her mental block.

Finally, she decided to call her mom, who immediately sensed Jenny's frustration.

"The first thing you need to do is clear your head. You need to stop what you're doing and go for a walk," her mother urged.

"But—"

"I know you're under the gun, but a change of scenery will help you unwind. And don't forget to ask God for help."

Going against her inclination, Jenny took her mother's advice. The sound of the birds was the first thing to get her attention, then the gentle spring breeze. As she walked, she took several deep breaths, and as she exhaled, a calm began to come over her.

"Father, I'm at the end of my rope with this project. I've been trying to do it in my own ability, and I need Your help."

As she was beginning to relax, she was finally able to isolate her main point and even a couple of other ideas. It was just a beginning, and she still had a lot of work ahead; but Jenny knew God had brought these thoughts into focus. As she returned home, Jenny began again with a clearer head and a renewed confidence that God would continue to help.

~

The help you need is only a prayer away.

Let us then approach the throne of grace with confidence, so that we may receive mercy and find grace to help us in our time of need.

Hebrews 4:16

37

If I had known what trouble you were bearing;
What griefs were in the silence of your face;
I would have been more gentle and more caring,
And tried to give you gladness for a space.

A Little Help from a Friend

Joni was a teacher's assistant in her daughter Katie's kindergarten class. Overall the class was filled with active but well-behaved children, except for Taylor. She couldn't seem to control herself and was often disruptive. She had difficulty getting along with the other children, and even Joni found her difficult to like. As a last resort, Taylor was seated at a table by herself instead of in groups like the rest of the children.

Realizing that the teacher of such a large class was not able to give Taylor individualized attention, Joni decided to "adopt" Taylor in the classroom. After clearing it with the

teacher, Joni learned that Taylor suffered from ADD and that her parents had recently divorced.

During seatwork time in class, Joni often sat with Taylor, overseeing her work and offering help where needed. She also made it a point to meet and reach out to Taylor's mother, offering compassionate support. When the mother was comfortable with Joni, she agreed to let Taylor go home with them one afternoon a week to play.

Taylor's difficulties were not reversed overnight, but slowly she began to respond. And Taylor was not the only one to benefit. Joni's daughter made a new friend and learned an important lesson in reaching out to others.

Inside each oyster is the potential for a pearl.

The LORD is gracious and righteous;
our God is full of compassion.

PSALM 116:5

The only people, scientific or other,
who never make mistakes
are those who do nothing.

Oops

Bill received his copy of the newsletter at the office. The mailroom had sent out eight hundred thousand, and Bill was feeling good about it. He had only been at the pharmaceutical company for a month, and the newsletter was his first big assignment. As he looked at the front page, he broke into a cold sweat. The headline was to read, "A Letter from Our President, Don T. Hinkle." Instead the CEO's name read "Tinkle"—the *H* being mistyped as a *T*. And the subject of Mr. "Tinkle's" letter? A break-through medication to aid in bladder control.

Bill knew he had to tell his boss but was especially apprehensive since he was new to the job. The boss was also responsible for proofreading the newsletter, but ultimately it was Bill's responsibility. He approached his boss, handed him the newsletter, then braced for the fallout.

The boss pondered the error. Then he looked up at Bill and began to laugh, "Guess we both missed that one," he said. "I'll apologize to Mr. *Tinkle.*"

"I'm really sorry about this," Bill said.

"Hey, mistakes happen; I should have caught it too," his boss said. "I'm sure we'll both be more careful next time."

Admit mistakes.
Forgive mistakes.
Then move on.

I have swept away your offenses like a cloud.

ISAIAH 44:22

41

Jesus knows we must come apart
and rest awhile, or else
we may just plain come apart.

Sacred Rest

Having some sort of monetary game plan for necessities like food, clothing, and shelter is an accepted practice. But what about budgeting time and resources for leisure? Is taking time out for R and R any less vital to our sense of well-being? Rest and rejuvenation are key components to living a full and rich life. How can we shine with the light of Christ if our own candle within has been extinguished through burnout?

Our loving Creator cares so strongly about this aspect of our lives that He included it in the Ten Commandments: "Six days you shall labor and do all your work, but the seventh day is a Sabbath to the Lord your God. On it you shall not do any work" (Exodus 20:9-10). The passage goes on to say that even the Lord himself rested on the seventh day after completing Creation.

What sounds restful to you? Is it curling up and reading a good book? Perhaps it is taking a stroll at a scenic location in your town. Or maybe you need to get away to unwind. Whatever the case, taking time out for yourself is not a luxury. It's an essential facet of life that will keep you burning brightly as you live life to the fullest.

~

Giving yourself time to rest will help you be your very best.

Jesus said, "Come to me, all you who are weary and burdened, and I will give you rest."

MATTHEW 11:28

43

At the heart of the cyclone tearing the sky
And flinging the clouds and the towers by,
Is a place of central calm;
So here in the roar of mortal things,
I have a place where my spirit sings,
In the hollow of God's palm.

Calming the Storm Within

Ever feel stressed out—stretched to your limit? Ever experience so much pressure that you feel like you're going to blow a gasket? Perhaps you feel that way today. Maybe the inner turmoil has become a raging tempest, threatening to take you under.

Jesus understands. When His disciples feared for their lives during a great storm, Jesus came to their rescue. And although the passage refers to the literal weather, we can apply the same principles to our inclement emotions.

44

Ideally we can learn to face inner storms the same way that Jesus did. His trust in His Father was so fully developed, that He was able to peacefully sleep through the wind and waves. Maybe a good night's rest, putting our cares into His hands, would be sufficient to gain perspective.

Or maybe it is easier to relate to the disciples' need for the Master's intervention. Meditating on the image of Jesus calming your personal storm may be just what the doctor ordered. Either way, it is "the mind controlled by the spirit" that is life and peace (Romans 8:6).

Jesus is our Prince of Peace, continually offering the gift of tranquility. Let Him restore the stillness to your stormy sea today.

Jesus still calms storms today.

[Jesus] arose, and rebuked the wind, and said unto the sea,
"Peace, be still." And the wind ceased,
and there was a great calm.

MARK 4:39 KJV

Nothing with God can be accidental.

Coincidences?

Dale and Karen woke up to a major drain leak in their only tub, just one in a series of minor catastrophes that had beset them since they had put their house on the market. Karen convinced Dale that they should take a break from their woes and go out for breakfast. As they walked into the café, the discouraged husband said, "Where are we ever going to find a plumber who will come over this weekend and not charge an arm and a leg?"

As they were seated, they overhead a man speaking in a Scottish brogue. Dale had spent some time in the United Kingdom and struck up a conversation with the man. As it turned out, this fellow had a friend who was a plumber. That afternoon, the Scotsman's friend came to their house and fixed the leak for a very reasonable cost.

As it turned out, the plumber and his family had been looking for a house to buy, so the next day he brought his wife and child back to the house. They put a contract on it the following day. What's more, the couples have become good friends over the fifteen years they've known each other and have even witnessed the marriages of each other's eldest children.

~

There's no such thing
as a coincidence in the
life of a Christian.

We know that in all things God works
for the good of those who love him,
who have been called according to his purpose.

ROMANS 8:28

God grant me the serenity
To accept the things I cannot change,
The courage to change the things I can,
And the wisdom to know
One from the other.

The Path of Peace

Dayna, a medical writer, was struggling to keep it together. She was seven months pregnant and several pounds heavier than she had been at the *end* of her previous pregnancy. Her two-year-old was taking the "terrible twos" to new heights, and she had just moved into a new house—and had yet to unpack. She felt a hint of sanity when she hired a young teenager to watch her son that afternoon, so she could conduct research for an article.

When the babysitter's mother called to say that the teen was sick, Dayna simply lowered herself onto the couch and sat. Then she began to sort through her extensive "to do" list for the absolute essentials: I have to carry this baby until he's born. I have to take care of my son. Eventually, I have to unpack.

But, I don't *have* to do this article. Normally hyperconscientious, she picked up the phone with some anxiety, not knowing how the editor would respond to her decision. Fifteen minutes later, however, she had been released from the burden, and sanity began to emerge. She made herself a cup of tea, went outside, and kicked back to watch her son play. She chose the most important thing. It was a day well spent.

Distinguishing between the have to's
and the can-waits can save a day.

Happy are those who find wisdom,
and those who get understanding, . . .
Her ways are ways of pleasantness,
and all her paths are peace.

PROVERBS 3:13-17 NRSV

A sense of humor is the pole that adds balance
to our steps as we walk the tightrope of life.

Easy to Please

Jane prepared to visit her friend Alexandria in Colorado Springs. She had heard of the beauty of Pikes Peak, so when Alexandria asked her what she'd like to do when she visited, Jane said, "I'd like to see Pikes Peak."

Alexandria said, "Oh, you want to go to the top of Pikes Peak?"

"Oh, no," Jane said, "just see it."

Alexandria muffled a chuckle and said intensely, "Well, I guess so. If that's what you want to do." Jane wondered if she had made an inappropriate request—she'd talk with her friend when she arrived.

As Jane's plane began its decent, the pilot announced, "Over to the west is Pikes Peak." Jane turned to her window and laughed as she quickly realized

the towering fourteen-thousand-foot mountain could be seen from nearly any vantage point in the city.

Jane not only saw the mountain, but ascended it as well. The two had a good laugh over what an easy-to-please guest Jane had been—a joke that continued for years to come.

Laughter is one of God's greatest gifts, a gift He shared with no other creature but man. When shared with a friend, combined with an ability to laugh at oneself, laughter is the glue that cements happy memories with those we love.

A good laugh with a friend is one
of life's greatest pleasures.

The cheerful heart has a continual feast.

Proverbs 15:15

Life let us cherish, while yet the taper glows.

Experience the Moment

Anyone who's getting married, having a baby, or preparing for any of the major life events will undoubtedly hear plenty of advice. On one such occasion as a young woman planned her wedding, she received some advice that was a real gem. It was a bit of advice from her boss that she took not only to her wedding day, but into the rest of her life.

Her boss said, "This day will never come again. The minute you wake up on your wedding day, stop and take a few minutes to really experience it. What does it smell like? Feel like? Look like? Before you walk down that aisle, engage every sense in the moment. Notice the individuals who have come to celebrate with you. Take a good look at the man you are about to marry. Taste your meal, your wedding cake. Make sure you consciously live and experience the day you've worked so hard to make special, instead of allowing it to become a blur."

Throughout our lives, God grants us many special moments that He means for us to enjoy to the fullest. Whether it's a special occasion, the "firsts" of your children, or times spent with family or friends, engage your senses! These times will never come again.

~

As you walk through the garden of life, don't forget to stop and smell the roses.

Jesus said, "I have come that they may have life, and have it to the full."

JOHN 10:10

Plenteous grace with Thee is found,
Grace to cover all my sins;
Let the healing streams abound,
Make and keep me pure within.

Good News

A Swedish chainsaw manufacturer decided to market his product in the U.S.—with an owner's manual that was considerably larger than the Swedish version. Swedish news commentators explained, tongue in cheek, that this was because of all the additional warnings including, "Do not attempt to stop the chainsaw with your hand."

This is laughable, but how many times do we ignore the simplest instructions given to us by our Father? Things like not eating too much, not gossiping, and not telling even "white" lies. These are certainly not laughable; however, they are basic instructions that we would do well to honor. Just like stopping a chainsaw with one's hand results in injury, spiritual guidelines are given to us to prevent injury to ourselves and others.

Instead of having a joyous, carefree spirit, we become weighted down each time we go against the grain of God's Word. However, there is good news! We don't have to carry the burden of guilt when we err. We can be forgiven and set free from sin's entanglement! First John 1:9 NASB states, "If we confess our sins, He is faithful and righteous to forgive us our sins and to cleanse us from all unrighteousness."

Feeling weighed down by guilt today? Your liberty is only a prayer away.

~

Stay clean on the inside—
shower often in the forgiveness of God.

By the blood of Christ we are set free, that is, our sins are forgiven. How great is the grace of God, which he gave to us in such large measure!

EPHESIANS 1:7-8 GNT

There are no ordinary people.

Significant Others

Technology affords many ways to stay in touch with others, yet how many of us feel we are too busy to even make the effort? If we aren't careful, we may lose our sense of connectedness to the people we love.

Although each is important, not all the people we know share the same level of significance. Every individual can be likened to a puzzle piece in the overall picture of our lives. Some, like our children and spouses, are few in number but act as the corner pieces to anchor the puzzle. With these people, there is no substitute for spending abundant quality time together.

Our extended family and circle of friends are like the straight-edged pieces of the puzzle, forming a solid perimeter. An occasional visit, phone call, or lunch out may be in order to keep these relationships intact.

Even a quick e-mail can be enough to maintain a connection until you can get together in person.

The other people in our lives are greater in number and can be likened to the majority of puzzle pieces. Not one is insignificant, because if even one piece is missing, the picture is incomplete.

Take some time to reevaluate. With whom would you like to connect today?

When it comes to the people we know, each is a significant other.

I thank my God every time I remember you.

PHILIPPIANS 1:3

A friend is one who
knows you as you are
understands where you've been
accepts who you've become
and still, gently invites you to grow.

Silver and Gold

"Make new friends but keep the old, one is silver and the other is gold." You may have learned the familiar lyrics in Girl Scouts, but the older we get, the more we realize just how true those words are. Mutual circumstances are often the catalyst through which new friendships are formed. It is refreshing to discover others who are in the same chapter of life that you are, whether it is a mom of one of your child's teammates or someone with whom you share a similar trial, such as the death of someone you love. It is encouraging to realize that you are not the only one who has suffered the thing you are going through, and it gives you an opportunity to focus your energy on encouraging others, instead of wallowing in the pain alone.

Let's not forget the friendships that have withstood the test of time. In friendships like these, participants give each other room to grow, and acceptance and forgiveness are prominent characteristics. These friendships are indeed as priceless as purest gold. So remember, it is important to continue investing time and energy to keep them alive.

Silver or gold? Which one of these treasures could use some polishing today?

~

Sharing life with friends
makes the journey sweeter.

Two are better than one. . . . For if they fall,
one will lift up the other; but woe to one who is
alone and falls and does not have another to help.

ECCLESIASTES 4:9–10 NRSV

Every person's life is a plan of God.

Greater Plan

In John Irving's book, *A Prayer for Owen Meaney*, Owen is a boy who believes God is preparing him for something special. His odd, strained-sounding voice is small for his age, and he has odd mannerisms. He doesn't hold to the convention around him and does what he believes to be right. As it turns out, Owen does have an important job to do—and when the time comes, he is prepared.

Some people seem certain of their mission in life. Others have no clue as to what special purpose God might have for them. But we can be certain that God has a purpose for each of our lives. It's not incumbent upon us to try to discover what it is, whether it's a very specific job or, more likely, a series of events in which we play an integral part. What is important is that we remain open to what God may want to accomplish in our lives. This openness can be expressed through prayer. We can ask for God's direction. We can ask Him to give us the strength of spirit to rest in whatever His will may be. We can then live in peace, knowing that God is sovereign, that His purpose will be worked out in His time.

~

An open mind and a submitted
heart are avenues through
which God fulfills His plans.

*"I know the plans I have for you," declares the LORD,
"plans to prosper you and not to harm you,
plans to give you hope and a future."*

JEREMIAH 29:11

Angels and ministers of grace defend us.

Angels in Our Midst

Mark rode shotgun in a car with his wife, Gretchen, and another couple, Tucker and Rhonda. The two men sat in front and the two women rode in the back. They were all in their early '60s and had been friends for years. It was a chilly December day, not one that would inspire a trip to the park or a stroll down a windy city street. The four finished shopping downtown and were off to dinner at a restaurant a few blocks down the road. As the car stopped for a red light, Mark had a sudden urge to jump from the car. He said, "I'll walk to the restaurant. Meet you there!" And he took off down the block.

The people left in the car couldn't imagine what had come over him. Tucker began to drive into the intersection. From nowhere a car slammed into the front side door on the passenger side. The door smashed inward,

62

and the front windshield shattered, spilling glass onto the front passenger's seat. No one in the car was hurt. When Mark realized what had happened, he was certain that God—or an angel—had saved him.

We can't necessarily see God or His angels working in our lives in such an obvious way. Nevertheless, they are in our midst. In everything you do, ask God for His protection. Thank Him for it and remember that there are indeed angels in our midst.

Know that you are never far
from God's watchful care.

*He will command his angels concerning
you to guard you in all your ways.*

PSALM 91:11

Is your place a small place?

Tend it with care!—He set you there.

Is your place a large place?

Guard it with care!—He set you there.

Whate'er your place, it is

Not yours alone, but his

Who set you there.

Taking Care of Business

The Barnards were having problems with their septic tank. Things had been backing up a bit, so they called the local specialists to assess and hopefully fix the situation. Jim and Jimmie Ray Jr. were southern boys who had been in the business for many years. Jimmie Ray pried the heavy concrete lid off the septic tank. "Grease!" he exclaimed. There was a layer of grease that could have plugged the Rio Grande.

"When was the last time you had this septic pumped?" asked Jim Sr.

"Pumped?" asked Mr. Barnard. "I didn't realize that the tank required that. We've only lived here a year, and the previous owners didn't say anything about it."

"Yes sir, these tanks need to be flushed every two years, and by the looks of it, this baby hasn't been pumped in at least fifteen," said Jimmie Ray as he began removing the years of accumulation.

The Barnard's neglect was unintentional. Thankfully, they caught the problem before serious damage occurred. Like their tank, there are many things in our lives that require regular maintenance if they are to work properly. Has your marriage had a tune-up lately? What about your relationship with a parent or a lifelong friend? Don't put it off. Why not schedule a "checkup" today?

~

Maintenance keeps things flowing freely.

The Lord God placed the man in the Garden of Eden as its gardener, to tend and care for it.

GENESIS 2:15 TLB

A bend in the road is not the end of the road,
unless you fail to make the turn.

A Change in Plans

Sarah planned a much-needed getaway for herself and her husband. They loved outdoor activities and decided to enjoy a weekend of hiking in the mountains. She made a reservation at a quaint bed and breakfast and could hardly wait to go.

Then came the head cold. To make matters worse, she and her husband got into a tiff that threatened to abort the affair altogether. That's when Sarah got a hold of herself. Realizing she had a choice to make, she determined to make things right with her husband and to load up on vitamin C and a decongestant.

"Mark, I'm sorry I got so upset. I've let myself get too stressed out, and my head is pounding."

"I'm sorry too. Are you sure you still want to go?"

"Absolutely. I don't feel too great, but I'm not going to let a silly head cold rob us of this time away."

So, armed with plenty of tissues and medication, the two set out for their special rendezvous. Instead of a bunch of rigorous activities, they enjoyed the mountain view from the porch of the B and B. The rest and relaxation were just what the doctor ordered, and the two returned home rejuvenated and ready to face the world again.

Don't be robbed of blessings.
Stay flexible and make
necessary adjustments.

The mind of man plans his way,
But the LORD directs his steps.
PROVERBS 16:9 NASB

Christ is the master;
the Scriptures are only the servant.

Words to Live By

A ninety-two-year-old woman said to her granddaughter, "I've been thinking about my life and why I've been given so many years here on earth. I don't think it is a coincidence," she continued, "that when I was eleven, my mother gave me a Bible. She opened it to Psalm 91 and told me to memorize it. The words have come to mind often during my life. Lord knows I've needed them. 'If you make the Most High your dwelling—even the LORD, who is my refuge—then no harm will befall you, no disaster will come near your tent.'" (Psalm 91:9-10).

Although she was not proud of it, this Bible-believing granny had been known around town for her lead foot—and a few car accidents in which, thankfully, no one was hurt, including herself. Once, she even flipped her car on a road trip through the desert of Arizona and didn't sustain a scratch. In spite of her poor driving record, she always came out unscathed. "I've had to ask God to forgive me for my reckless driving, but then I just keep on praying that psalm and thanking God for His protection."

"He will call upon me, and I will answer him; I will be with him in trouble, I will deliver and honor him" (v. 15). This and many other Psalms provide a wonderful means of prayer, and those prayers really do affect our lives.

God watches over His Word
to perform it.

The LORD said to me, "You have seen correctly,
for I am watching to see that my word is fulfilled."

JEREMIAH 1:12

Work and play are an artificial pair of opposites
because the best kind of play contains an element
of work, and the most productive kind of work
must include something of the spirit of play.

The Rhythm of Life

Picture a rocking chair on a porch on a mild summer day. Add a good book and a glass of lemonade, and you have the ingredients for a perfect day, right? What if you were to sit there all day every day, rocking but going nowhere?

On the other hand, imagine a palm organizer, a laptop computer, and a cell phone. They could represent a workaholic who has no time for his wife and children, or they could be tools to enable the businessperson to work more efficiently, so they have more time with their family. Whether these things are a blessing or a curse depends on how they are used.

A symphony is made up of a vast array of instruments. A composition involving only a double bass would be pretty dull, but when combined with the other instruments, it offers richness and depth to the sound of the whole.

Temperance is a sign of a person who has learned the rhythm of life. Moderation is an important key to whether we are living a life of excess and pain or the abundant life Jesus intended—well balanced and fulfilling.

Often small adjustments are all that is needed to keep life on track. Could you use a little tweaking to restore balance to your life?

~

Moderation keeps life in balance.

Let your gentleness be evident to all.

PHILIPPIANS 4:5

71

It is good news, worthy of all acceptation;
and yet not too good to be true.

Good News!

A little boy often accompanied his grandpa to the beach in Rhode Island. His grandfather had been a drinkin', brawlin' Marine. He had a pretty rough go of it. One day, the man came to see that he couldn't go it alone, and he "found religion." His life was so changed that he wanted everyone to know the Good News.

This grandfather walked the beach with Bible tracts, giving sunbathers and surfers a line that the little boy would never forget. The man would say, "You read about bad news all the time in the papers. How would you like to read about the Good News?" He would then hand them a tract that explained salvation through Jesus Christ. The grandfather had something good to share, something he knew would make a difference in people's lives and bring them lasting hope.

When looking at the newspapers, TV, and tabloids, we find that good news is in short supply. We've become a culture that almost expects the negative, and many of us have become cynical, speaking negatively ourselves. Why not focus more on the good, the inspiring—those things that have really made a difference in our lives—and then let others in on our good news.

God is good, and everything about Him is good news.

I bring you good news of great joy for everyone!

LUKE 2:10 NLT

For one man who can introduce another to
Jesus Christ by the way he lives and by the
atmosphere of his life, there are a thousand
who can only talk jargon about him.

Living Testimony

There is nothing more beautiful than the life of a
believer who allows Christ to live through them.
Margaret was one of those people. From the moment
people met her, they were put at ease. She was the kind of
person you felt you had known all your life. Many would
say she was an "open book." And why not? Margaret's was
a life totally dedicated and yielded to her
Lord and Savior, and the light ema-
nating from her was testimony to
that fact. People—even complete
strangers—were drawn to her,
like a moth to a flame.

How did she do it? She'd tell
you it was no secret. Every
morning she would simply talk

74

to her Father, saying, "Lord, today I yield myself to You. I yield my mind to think Your thoughts, my tongue to speak Your words. May my actions be Yours working through me."

Margaret was "Jesus" to everyone with whom she came into contact. Actions indeed speak louder than words, and Margaret's life made a bold statement of faith and the new life that Christ provides. This is the essence of the Christian life. The apostle Paul referred to believers as letters that are known and read by all men. What do people "read" when they meet you?

Actions speak louder than any sermon can.

You yourselves are our letter, written on our hearts, known and read by everybody.

2 CORINTHIANS 3:2

Every end is a new beginning.

Smooth Transitions

"I have had to totally change my thinking," Wendy said to Jeff, her husband, who was laid off a couple of months earlier. After searching diligently for work, he realized that the only opportunities in his field were out of state. Jeff and Wendy both had family in town and had always pictured their children growing up near aunts, uncles, cousins, and familiar friends. Yet clearly the best options for career and earning potential were elsewhere.

In one way or another, many of us experience similar unsettling situations. We set our minds on a particular path, only to find that it leads in a direction different from what we had imagined or intended. How we handle these transitions depends largely on in whom we place our trust.

People and circumstances often change, but Jesus Christ is a firm foundation who remains constant and never changes. When we allow Him to become the anchor of our souls, we can be confident that His plans for us are good and full of blessing. We may be able to see only the next step ahead, but He promises to guide us and take us to "a land flowing with milk and honey" (Exodus 3:8).

Jesus is a reliable guide,
helping us make transitions smoothly.

We fix our eyes not on what is seen,
but on what is unseen. For what is seen
is temporary, but what is unseen is eternal.

2 CORINTHIANS 4:18

A successful marriage is not a gift;
it is an achievement.

What's Your Type?

A person's temperament plays a large role in how they approach life. Understanding these temperaments is helpful in knowing ourselves and relating to those closest to us. Danny and Shelly had been married only about six months, yet they found their "honeymoon period" had far fewer challenges than expected during their first year of marriage. What accounted for their marital bliss?

Danny and Shelly attributed their easy adjustment to the in-depth premarital counseling they received and a commitment to communicate. They learned that a person's temperament doesn't confine them to a particular "box," but it does act as a filter through which one sees and responds to the world. Danny immediately recognized himself as the fun-loving extrovert, who takes life as it comes. Shelly, on the other hand, was obviously more introverted with a strong sense of right and wrong and an appreciation for a more structured lifestyle.

So how did these two opposites ever find common ground? "The main thing is that we have tried to see life through the other person's eyes and have made it a point to meet in the middle. We strive for win/win situations where we are both comfortable."

Does this lifestyle take work? Yes, of course, but Danny and Shelly have found that the rewards are well worth the effort.

∾

Opposites attract, but working together creates harmony.

If the whole body were an eye,
where would the sense of hearing be?

1 CORINTHIANS 13:17

Cheerful company shortens the miles.

About Face; Forward March

"I'm tired of being overweight and out of shape," announced Jill to her friend Gina. "I've never lost the extra weight from my pregnancies, and I'm finally ready to do something about it."

"Why the sudden resolve?" inquired Gina.

"I caught a glimpse of myself in the mirror and didn't like what I saw. Besides, now that my children are all in school, I can use the extra time to get back into shape," shared Jill.

Jill determined to go on a rigorous thirty-minute walk, five days each week. Gina also decided that she could stand to lose a few pounds, so the two committed to walk together. After a couple of weeks, the pair decided to change their snacking habits from chips and cookies to fresh fruit, nuts, and seeds. They also began to serve their families salads and to cut back on fried foods. The changes took some getting used to, but over time, both women—and their families—began to benefit.

Most activities are more enjoyable when shared with a friend. Is it time for you to make a change? How about phoning a friend to see if they are interested too. You'll be happy with the changes you see, and it will be a whole lot more fun, sharing your success with a friend.

Friends make even the
dullest activity more fun.

As iron sharpens iron,
so one man sharpens another.
PROVERBS 27:17

He has achieved success who has lived well,
laughed often, and loved much.

When Conscientiousness Becomes Obsession

xcellence. It's a term we hear often, especially in the career world. By nature, most of us desire to do a good job at the things we do, whether it is parenting or climbing the corporate ladder. But when does conscientiousness become obsession?

Conscientious means "meticulous, painstaking." *Obsessed* means "preoccupied intensely or abnormally."[1] From childhood, we are drilled to do our best. Whether it's to make an *A* on an algebra test or to break the school record in a track meet, it is part of our nature to want to win.

But when does conscientiousness cross the line and become obsession? When does perfectionism cease to be a blessing and become a curse? When it begins to interfere with other aspects of our lives. When this happens, it is a signal that we need to step back and reevaluate our priorities. *Is this a price I am willing to pay? Or can I do excellent work that exceeds expectations, yet still give needed attention to other important areas of my life?*

Of course these are questions each person must ask himself. As in most things, moderation is the key. Excellence is a coveted trait. Keeping it in balance with our relationships and other areas of life is the secret to true success.

Keeping priorities in line is part of the excellent life.

God looked over all that he had made, and it was excellent in every way.

GENESIS 1:31 TLB

---

[1] *Merriam-Webster's Collegiate Dictionary*, Electronic Edition, Version 1.2; copyright 1994-6, Merriam Webster Inc.

Words—so innocent and powerless as they are,
as standing in a dictionary, how potent for
good and evil they become, in the hands
of one who knows how to combine them!

Gossip-Free Zone

Amy has hosted the sewing club on Wednesday afternoons for years. The ladies have met since their children were little. Most of their children are in college now, but the sewing club ladies still meet. Although they did sew, the main draw for the women remained social.

Amy had grown concerned over the past year that the club had become too catty. When one of the women would bring up the new church deacon or so-and-so's nephew in order to discuss the latest intrigue, Amy tried to find a diplomatic way to reroute the conversation, usually to no avail. The demand for good gossip remained high. Finally, Amy decided to take action against the moral direction of the sewing club. At the next club meeting, Amy announced that from then on, the sewing club was a gossip-free zone.

"It's the only way I can think of to keep our conversation positive and uplifting. None of us means to speak ill of others, but it is a habit we can easily slip into. If we all work on this, though, I think we can turn the atmosphere of our get-togethers around." It did take time, but before too long, the sewing club once again became a place of blessing and kind words.

~

You never have to worry about
good words getting back
to the wrong person.

Let your conversation be always full of
grace, seasoned with salt, so that you
may know how to answer everyone.

COLOSSIANS 4:6

85

You are not accepted by God because
you deserve to be, or because
you have worked hard for him;
but because Jesus died for you.

The Road to Freedom

A sense of inadequacy can eat away like a slow-growing cancer. Most often it comes through one's thoughts. One thought whispers, *You can't do anything right.* Another shouts, *Not good enough.* Still another says, *You'll never amount to anything,* accompanied by name-calling—*Idiot, Loser*—enslaving its victim.

Even sadder, many believe that those thoughts are the voice of God condemning them, saying, "You don't measure up." The enemy of your soul, the devil, would love for you to believe that. In truth, God knows none of us can measure up! "For *all* have sinned and fall short of the glory of God, and are justified freely by his grace through the redemption that came by Christ Jesus" (Romans 3:23-24). God is also the one who changes you for the better, from the inside out, as you spend time with Him—that too is a gift.

Believing that God loves you just the way you are is the first step toward freedom. Then loving yourself and accepting yourself, just the way you are, is the next step. Only then can you take the third step of loving others just the way they are. Step-by-step you will find yourself well on your way to a lifelong journey of freedom in Christ.

~

There is freedom in accepting God's grace—freedom to live, freedom to love ourselves, and freedom to love others without reserve.

It is for freedom that Christ has set us free.
Stand firm, then, and do not let yourselves
be burdened again by a yoke of slavery.

GALATIANS 5:1

There are, in everyone's life, certain connections,
twists, and turns which pass awhile under
the category of chance, but at the last,
well examined, prove to be the very hand of God.

The Hand of God

Brad was at the height of his career, but instead of receiving the promotion he had worked so hard for, he received a layoff notice—effective immediately. He was shocked and hurt after having given his all to the company and was tempted to be angry at God. Knowing that this was fruitless, Brad and his wife, Pam, came together in prayer and made a conscious decision to trust God to see them through.

Soon Brad's friend Max, who had been in the same situation the year before, called. Knowing from personal experience what his friend was going through, Max offered to take Brad to lunch, where he gave Brad some job leads and an understanding shoulder to lean on. He insisted they meet weekly until Brad landed his next job.

Some other buddies insisted he play golf with them—their treat. Their daughter's preschool happened to have an emergency fund for situations like theirs, and Megan never missed a day. They even received a hefty gift certificate for groceries. The generosity of others continued to come their way, until Brad found his new job.

Receiving from others is indeed a humbling experience, but through their actions we see the hand of God.

~

God's helping hand often looks like your next-door neighbor's.

God has said,
"Never will I leave you;
never will I forsake you."
So we say with confidence,
"The Lord is my helper; I will not be afraid."
HEBREWS 13:5-6

It is one of the beautiful compensations
of this life that no one can sincerely try
to help another without helping himself.

Fill It Up

An energetic woman scurries down the hall, a bottle of glass cleaner in her hand and a smile on her face. She has been there for ten years as a volunteer—working with the terminally ill. This did not come naturally to Audrey. In fact, the sick and elderly had made her uncomfortable until her own mother was dying. Through the help of hospice care, Audrey, her mother, and the rest of the family received priceless support as they navigated through the final months of her mother's life.

After her mother's death, there was a void in Audrey's heart. Then one day she happened to run into one of the hospice counselors who mentioned that they needed volunteers. Instantly, Audrey knew that this was the perfect way to fill the empty spot and, at the same time, to be a great blessing to others going through what she and her family had.

Although her official job has been to keep the place sparkling, she has eagerly helped the nurses and offered support to the patients and their family members. "I shine a mirror, pour some water, have a conversation. Truth is, I keep coming because I get so much more than I give."

Do you have a void that could be filled by helping another?

～

When you give, you can't help but receive.

"It is more blessed to give than to receive."

ACTS 20:35

A saint is one the light shines through.

Light That Comes from Within

The children of Elm Hills Elementary School adored their principal, Dr. Parsons, a tall gangly man with a southern drawl that delighted the children. Dr. Parsons spent as much time as he could visiting the different classrooms. Even the teachers looked forward to Dr. Parsons' visits. He emanated a warmth and kindness that was infectious to everyone.

Most of the children who graduated from Elm Hills remember Dr. Parsons clearly, not only because he was their principal, but also because he made such a strong impression on them. To this day, former students send him Christmas cards—even after he retired. Dr. Parsons is a man of great faith, but he doesn't talk about it often. Rather, he makes his faith known by the love and light that shine from his inner being. His actions speak much louder than any words he could ever say.

Coffee Break Devotions: Latte

So what about the light in your heart? Is it brightening the lives of those in your world? If not, the Holy Spirit is only a prayer away to blow upon the embers of your soul and get the flame burning brightly again.

You are the light of the world.

"You are the light of the world . . .
Let your light shine before men,
that they may see your good deeds
and praise your Father in heaven."

You can never change the past. But by the grace of God, you can win the future. So remember those things which will help you forward, but forget those things which will only hold you back.

New Things

Leigh was an elementary-school teacher and a single mother of two young daughters. It wasn't easy to make it on her salary, but the schedule was compatible and provided stability, as did their faith in God.

One fall, Leigh had a little boy in her class who had recently lost his mother. Naturally, Leigh felt compassion for the boy and always made it a point to offer the child a little extra attention when he needed it, even helping him after hours with his homework. During their parent/teacher conference, the boy's father, John, expressed his appreciation to Leigh. As it turned out, the boy spoke of "Miss Roberts" often to his father, and it was obvious that she was a healing influence in his life.

Leigh looked more and more forward to seeing John every morning when he dropped off his son. Their chats were brief; but they shared a common faith, and it became apparent that John, also, anticipated their encounters. At the end of the school year, John expressed his desire to get to know Leigh and her girls on a more personal basis, and that summer the two families spent a considerable amount of time together, finally deciding to make the two families one.

~

In the midst of dark times,
remember the story's not over.

Forget the former things;
do not dwell on the past.
See, I am doing a new thing!
Now it springs up; do you not perceive it?

ISAIAH 43:18-19

95

*No problem is ever as dark when you
have a friend to face it with you.*

The Green, Green Grass
of Someone Else's Life

Gail's second child was three months old, and her first child was a demanding two-going-on-three-year-old who decided that he wanted to become potty-trained. While Gail was eager to get her son out of diapers, she felt overwhelmed from the sleep deprivation and multiple trips to the bathroom each day.

Meanwhile, Gail's best friend, Rachel, called to say hi. The two had been friends since college and were still close despite the fact their lives had taken very different turns. Rachel was single and had a high-powered career, but she had grown lonely from her frequent travels out of town on business.

As the two shared their woes, Rachel had an idea. "Gail, I'm going to be in town for a few days. Why don't I come over on my two days off and work with Tyler on the potty training? You know I adore him, and I could really use some 'family' time."

Gail, eagerly responded, "I have to cook dinner anyway, so why don't I cook that oriental recipe you like so much. I bet a home-cooked meal might taste good after all of that restaurant food."

Friendship is a mutually giving relationship. Is there a "Rachel" in your life with whom you could share your burdens? Why not give your friend a call today?

~

If the grass looks greener on the other side, why not offer to cut it!

By helping each other with your troubles, you truly obey the law of Christ.

GALATIANS 6:2 NCV

God is an ever-present Spirit guiding
all that happens to a wise and holy end.

Follow Your Gut

Kim finally saved enough to make a down payment on a house. After months of searching, she found a house that seemed perfect for her. It was part of a new development of patio homes, offered with the option to buy or rent. Kim prayed about the purchase and talked with people in the area. It was a great deal, right in her price range and had most of the amenities she desired. But when it came time to make an offer, something inside said, "*Rent.*" She felt she had found the home she was to move into, and although she didn't understand why, she chose to follow her gut. Those close to her were surprised that she would throw her money away on rent when she could have made a great investment.

A few weeks after she moved in, a heavy downpour descended. Instead of running off the roof, the rain came streaming into her living room, bath-room, and bedroom. One of the roofers the landlord hired to fix the leaks said, "Yeah, these houses have shoddy construction."

Kim knew when her lease was up, she would move on. What she didn't know at the time was that the bold roofer would ask her for a date and eventually, for her hand in marriage!

Pray, listen, and follow your instincts.

I will instruct you and teach you in the way you should go;
I will counsel you and watch over you.

PSALM 32:8

Let your holidays be associated with great public events, and they may be the life of patriotism as well as a source of relaxation.

Party On!

Milwaukee, Wisconsin, is a city that likes to celebrate. They host the cherry, apple, and cheese festivals, as well as the Irish, German, Italian, and Polish festivals. These festivals are excellent ways to unite the community and provide meaningful opportunities to celebrate special occasions, people groups, and seasons.

If you read through the Old Testament, it isn't long before you realize the Israelites commemorated everything from harvest time to the parting of the Red Sea. They passed down through generations these traditions, many of which are still celebrated today. And then there are birthday and anniversary parties, family and class reunions. So why all of this celebration?

Each of these occasions is a time set aside to celebrate and reflect on the wonderful things God has done in our lives. With all of the stress and challenges of day-to-day life, they help us to gain fresh perspective, to step back and see what is really important, and to give us the opportunity to express our thankfulness to a good and loving God.

So the next time you think you're too busy to take time for special celebrations, maybe you should think again. It might be just what you need. You might even have a good time!

~

There is always a reason to celebrate.

You are always to remember this day and celebrate it with a feast to the LORD. Your descendants are to honor the LORD with this feast from now on.

EXODUS 12:14 NCV

That they are never sated
makes all the saints rejoice;
Oh, what a happy hunger!
Oh, what a blessed thirst!

Could You Use a Drink?

Have you ever been *really* thirsty? Although most have never been stranded in the desert with nothing to drink, no doubt all of us have been so thirsty at one time or another that we'd pay a premium price just to get one sip of water. Think about the last time you were *that* thirsty and how it felt.

Now remember how you felt when you finally began to drink that nice, cold glass of water. Didn't it taste better than anything in the world?

Why all the imagery? To illustrate how very thirsty our souls are for just one drink of the living water that Jesus gives. We often mistake that thirst for a desire for something or someone. We think, *If I can just reach this goal or have this thing, then I'll be satisfied.* Only when we finally get that thing, we're still thirsty for more. The bottom line is, no earthly thing can satisfy the way that Jesus can.

Bet you're thirsty just thinking about this. Why not get yourself a nice, cold glass of water? As you begin to drink, also drink in the living water of God's presence. Bask in it awhile, and let it quench the thirst in your soul.

Ahhhh . . . isn't that refreshing!

Nothing satisfies the thirst of the soul like living water.

O God, you are my God,
earnestly I seek you;
my soul thirsts for you,
my body longs for you,
in a dry and weary land
where there is no water.

PSALM 63:1

IO3

I want people to be sincere; a man of honor
shouldn't speak a single word that
doesn't come straight from his heart.

Straight from the Heart

"Flattery will get you nowhere." It's a familiar adage. What's sad, however, is that flattery is so rampant and so many people use it to get them *every*where they want to go.

No mature person wants to be flattered, but everyone appreciates a sincere compliment. Isn't it refreshing to be around people who are sincere, who mean what they say and say what they mean? If they give you a compliment, you don't have to wonder if they really mean it. You know it's heartfelt, and it's a priceless gift when taken to heart.

Being a person of honor is one of the telltale signs of a true disciple of Jesus. Jesus was sincere. Everything He ever did

He did from His heart of boundless love. As His children, we have the privilege of doing the same. But it takes commitment on our part to be a person of integrity.

Want to be a blessing to others? Be quick to pay them a sincere compliment or acknowledge some wonderful quality you see in them. Talk might be cheap, but when sincere words are spoken straight from the heart, those words become precious gems to enrich the recipient.

Whose life could you enrich today?

Life-giving words come straight from the heart.

We will lovingly follow the truth at all times—speaking truly, dealing truly, living truly—and so become more and more in every way like Christ.

Ephesians 4:15-16 tlb

At the cross, at the cross
where I first saw the light,
And the burden of my heart rolled away,
It was there by faith I received my sight,
And now I am happy all the day!

I Saw the Light

In his book, *Space and Sight,* Marius von Senden describes the experience of people born blind who receive their sight after having undergone cataract surgery. Imagine as an adult seeing the beauty of a sunset for the very first time!

This dramatic experience has mental and spiritual parallels as well. Do you remember sitting in math class as a child, straining to understand how to do a math problem the teacher was explaining? Do you remember what it was like when the light finally came on and you "got it"? That feeling of triumph?

This "first sight" experience is what happens on a spiritual level when a person receives Jesus Christ as their

Lord and Savior. Suddenly their heart is flooded with light, and spiritual things take on new significance—life makes sense. As believers continue to pursue Him, more and more light is made available, giving God's children the wisdom and insight they need to live life to the full.

Is there an area of your life where you feel you're "in the dark"? Look to the Bible for the answers you seek. The Holy Spirit is available to you 24/7 to "turn on the light" and give you the wisdom you need.

∾

When Jesus is on the scene,
darkness takes a hike.

With thee is the fountain of life: In thy light we see light.

PSALM 36:9 KJV

Joy is distinctly a Christian word and a Christian thing. It is the reverse of happiness. Happiness is the result of what happens of an agreeable sort. Joy has its springs deep down inside. And that spring never runs dry, no matter what happens. Only Jesus gives that joy. He had joy, singing its music within, even under the shadow of the cross.

I've Got That Joy, Joy, Joy, Joy Down in My Heart

Everyone wants to be happy, and many in our culture are living life in the fast lane trying to get there. But happiness, based on circumstances, is short-lived. As soon as the new wears off or something goes awry, happiness is replaced by discontent or sadness. Life becomes a roller-coaster ride of ups and downs, but there is an alternative.

The "inexpressible joy" available to those who follow Jesus does not fluctuate wildly like happiness does. In contrast, its source in God is as constant as He is. And unlike happiness, joy can abound in the face of suffering and trials.

Although joy is not based on circumstances, there is plenty for the believer to be joyful about. Aside from the blessings of this life, Heaven is a real place, a place where there is no sorrow, no tears, and no pain. Not only that, it is a place where believers will enjoy a wonderful time of unbroken fellowship with those they love—no more good-byes.

The next time you feel unhappy—cheer up! Take your eyes off the thing making you blue, and refocus your gaze to see the big picture. Draw on the joy of the Lord and remember that nothing you are going through today can compare to the incomprehensible blessings that await you!

The joy of the Lord will never pass away.

You love him even though you have never seen him; though not seeing him, you trust him; and even now you are happy with the inexpressible joy that comes from heaven itself.

1 PETER 1:8 TLB

A rose can say I love you,
Orchids can enthrall,
But a weed bouquet in a chubby fist,
Oh my, that says it all!

Priceless

Anyone who has children knows the constant challenges of parenting. In fact, at times it is like out-and-out war as parents try to be consistent in their discipline and to channel all of that boundless energy. The responsibility alone is enough to overwhelm the faint of heart.

"So why have them?" some may ask. Puzzled by the question, parents know exactly why. Sure it's hard, but the rewards are priceless. Few things in life can compare to the joy of chubby hands clutching a bouquet of dandelions for Mom. Then there are the special rocks, the handmade Fruit-Loop bracelets, and the masterpieces scrawled in crayon or done in finger paints. And what about that cherubic face asleep on the pillow? The feel of that precious hand in yours? The scent of baby powder after a bath, the little freckles appearing on the nose, the sparkle in the eye when they ride their bike on their own, the squeals of laughter when tickled, the sound of "Hey Mommy?" And who could forget when they learn to read for the very first time?

Yes, children have a mind of their own, and they sometimes try their parent's last nerve. But the blessings far outweigh the difficulties, and the memories last forever.

Kodak moments are the stuff memories are made of.

Oh, how blessed are you parents,
with your quivers full of children!

PSALM 127:5 THE MESSAGE

To weep is to make less the depth of grief.

This, Too, Shall Pass

Different cultures deal with loss and grief in various ways. In the Jewish tradition, the immediate family observes a seven-day mourning period when a person passes away called *sitting Shiva*. During this time, the immediate family sits on the floor with one another for seven straight days. Each person tears a part of their clothing as a sign of mourning, and friends and family come to the house, bringing food and sharing in the time of mourning. Together they work through their grief, finding support in one another.

In the Western tradition, we often take a stoic approach to mourning. In fact, we praise those who are "strong" and refrain from outward expressions of grief. Most people don't know what to do with their grief. They are busy trying not to make others uncomfortable, and they feel miserable. They struggle with the desire to give vent to some very deep feelings.

Grief is a natural response to loss, and fighting it may actually increase one's feeling of sorrow. Giving oneself permission to grieve is the first step. Working through your grief with another can yield healing to both. Allowing God to comfort will make the way for joy to return once again.

~

Don't deny grief.
Let it pass on through.

Weeping may remain for a night,
but rejoicing comes in the morning.

PSALM 30:5

The happiest moments of my life have
been the few which I have passed
at home in the bosom of my family.

The Best Christmas Ever

In early 1983, Charles lost his job and found out he had cancer. Married with three children, he had no idea how to cope. By Christmas, he miraculously triumphed over his cancer, but he and his wife still faced the daunting task of getting through the holidays with three young children and no money.

Charles knew his children adored Christmas more than any other celebration. Their excitement began the moment their mother said it was time to get out the Christmas music. Late Christmas Eve, Charles surveyed the few gifts under the tree with a heavy heart. *They'll be so disappointed,* he thought. The next morning, as they opened each one of their presents, his children squealed with glee.

Each year, after all the presents were opened, his oldest daughter would say, "This is the best Christmas ever." This year, after she had opened all her gifts, his oldest daughter turned a very satisfied face to the rest of her family and said resolutely, "This is the best Christmas ever."

Years later, Charles asked each one of his children separately what it was they loved most about Christmas. Each one of them answered the same: the family being together.

～

The greatest joys in life
don't have to cost a dime.

"Where your treasure is,
there your heart will be also."

MATTHEW 6:21

A word, once let out of the cage,
cannot be whistled back again.

Time Out

"Go to your room!" Janice shouted. She didn't know who needed the time out more—her or her daughters. Her six- and twelve-year-old had been outside giving the dog a bath.

Just thirty minutes earlier, she instructed them, "Be sure to dry him off, but *don't let him back in the house.* He needs to stay outside until he gets completely dry."

Janice went back to doing the laundry. When the noise from the dryer stopped, she heard a commotion downstairs. Instantly, she knew.

As she entered the room, she gasped. Hundreds of muddy paw prints now adorned the light-colored carpet, and droplets of water were dripping down the walls and furniture. Boots was having a grand time as the younger daughter chased him around the room with the towel.

About that time, her older daughter, who had been on the phone, joined them, horrified.

As Janice ordered her daughters to their rooms, she slammed the door behind Boots as he scampered back outside. A scene from her childhood flashed into her mind. Her father's explosive temper had left scars, yet she had the same tendency.

Although she had yelled the command, she had the presence of mind to demand the much-needed time out. She had trained herself to separate herself from her girls until she could cool off and think clearly.

Of course the daughters were disciplined and lost some cherished privileges, but all was done calmly and in a non-threatening manner. The house was a mess, but Janice realized her victory.

You'll never regret the angry words you do not speak.

He who is slow to anger is better than the mighty,
And he who rules his spirit, than he who captures a city.

PROVERBS 16:32 NASB

The heart that is to be filled to the brim
with holy joy must be held still.

Cultivating Quiet

Hurry, hurry, hurry. Ever feel like you want to stop the merry-go-round you're on? Think of all the gadgets and technologies that have been invented to save us time and make our lives more efficient. The information superhighway is available at the push of a button, 24/7. You can even trade stocks with a click of a mouse. Answering machines screen our calls, allowing us to leave a quick message when a person is not home. Better yet, try to reach them on their cell phones or e-mail.

But what is the net result of all of these conveniences? Have they given us more free time? If you are like most, you have even less time than before.

Going with the flow is not difficult. The challenge lies in what we have to do—grab life by the horns and simply *stop!* Life does not stop for us, and we won't experience serenity unless we jump off the merry-go-round and take some time to be quiet. It's harder than you think, but the rewards are well worth it.

Next time you get home from running around in the car, take a couple of minutes to prop up your feet and experience the quiet. Don't give in to the temptation to turn on the TV or radio. Instead, go to the secret place of the Most High. Abide with the Prince of Peace, and see how refreshing it is.

~

The Shepherd of your soul is calling you to a quiet resting place.

My soul finds rest in God alone;
my salvation comes from him.

PSALM 62:1

God loves us not because of who
we are, but because of who He is.

i Love You!

"Love your neighbor as yourself" (Matthew 19:19). It's a familiar commandment, but often misunderstood. Most believers are well aware of the importance of loving others, putting them first. However, the second half of the sentence is often overlooked. There is a condition to loving others—as you love yourself!

When was the last time you looked yourself in the mirror and said, "I sure love you"? Chances are it's been awhile, if ever. Knowing ourselves as we do, we are conscious of our failures and shortcomings. Accepting ourselves, warts and all, is not always easy. But even this is not the first step.

"We love because He first loved us" (1 John 4:19). Receiving the love God has for us is the starting point for all relationships, including the relationship we have with ourselves. We can't give ourselves or anyone else something we don't have. But when we are filled up with God's love and accept His forgiveness, we have the grace to love ourselves and let ourselves off the hook for our failings. From there we can obey the commandment to love others, as we love ourselves.

~

Receiving God's love + loving ourselves = the ability to love others.

I pray that you, being rooted and established in love,
may have power, together with all the saints, to grasp
how wide and long and high and deep is the love of Christ,
and to know this love that surpasses knowledge—
that you may be filled to the measure
of all the fullness of God.

EPHESIANS 3:17-19

*The awareness of a need and the capacity
to meet that need: this constitutes a call.*

Go Ye into All the Earth

Barry had never given much thought to missions. He had not grown up in church and had never heard a missionary speak, although one was scheduled for the evening service. He hadn't been particularly interested and almost stayed home that night. At the last minute, he decided to go.

As the missionary approached the podium, Barry thought to himself, *That guy looks so . . . normal.* As the young man introduced his lovely wife and three children, Barry realized his preconceived idea about missionaries was inaccurate.

The missionary said several things Barry related to, but the thing that struck him most was his heart for souls. He spoke with an enthusiasm and conviction that Barry realized he lacked—but he wanted. As he watched a video narrated by the missionary, Barry's heart was stirred. Seeing the joy in the people's faces upon hearing the Gospel made an indelible impression in his heart.

At the conclusion of the missionary's presentation, he announced upcoming short-term medical missions trips. As a physician's assistant, Barry possessed the medical skills needed. But more than that, he wanted to experience for himself the thrill of leading hungry hearts to the Lord.

There are many ways to be involved in missions. You can go or you can send others. The world in which you live is a mission field in itself. Once you witness the joy of those accepting Christ, you'll be hooked for life.

Whether you go or send, missions is at the center of God's heart.

"I tell you, there is rejoicing in the presence of the angels of God over one sinner who repents."

Luke 15:10

The goodness of God knows how to use
our disordered wishes and actions, often
lovingly turning them to our advantage while
always preserving the beauty of his order.

God Is at Work

Pregnancy had been David and Heather's main desire for over five years. They had tried every conceivable method. They poured money into procedure after invasive procedure only to be disappointed time and again. Experiencing every form of grief, anger, frustration, sadness, and despair, they were on an emotional roller coaster. Eventually, they simply didn't have the strength or the funds to try anymore. They mourned the loss of a child they were never able to conceive.

Two years later, Heather flew home after visiting her parents. On the plane she noticed an uncanny number of babies crying. The stewardess announced that they had officially broken their airline's record for the most babies on board. All the babies, she reported, were little girls adopted from China. As she exited the plane, Heather gazed with intrigue at all of the parents joyfully embracing their new little daughters. Though others had suggested the idea of adoption, Heather hadn't felt ready to entertain the idea up to this point.

After she got home, she couldn't get those baby girls off of her mind. After talking with David, they decided to investigate Chinese adoption for themselves. Two years later, Heather and David returned home with the precious little girl they had traveled across the world to meet. Heather tearfully gazed at the baby sleeping in her arms and knew that this had been God's plan all along.

❧

Even when it doesn't look like it,
God is at work on your behalf.

How great is your goodness,
which you have stored up for those who fear you,
which you bestow in the sight of men
on those who take refuge in you.

PSALM 31:19

When the dream in our heart is one that God has planted there, a strange happiness flows into us. At that moment all of the spiritual resources of the universe are released to help us. Our praying is then at one with the will of God and becomes a channel for the Creator's always joyous, triumphant purposes for us and our world.

I Have a Dream

Around the turn of the twentieth century, a young mechanic who worked in a railroad shop in Salt Lake City, Utah, had big dreams. This young mechanic diligently saved, intending to start a business for himself. When he accumulated about four thousand dollars in savings, he decided to invest in the burgeoning automotive industry.

The young man shocked his family and friends when he spent every last penny of his savings on an automobile. They were even more shocked when he took his brand-new purchase apart until the entire thing lay in pieces on his garage floor. He then proceeded to put the car back together again, repeating the process several times, until he had everyone convinced that he truly had gone mad.

The young man observed every detail down to the last bolt, nut, and screw. He became intimately acquainted with the strong and weak points of the car. Eventually, after integrating all the strong points he observed in the car that he had dismantled and studied so many times, the young man designed and eventually produced a car that quickly became the hottest thing in the new automotive industry. The man went on to become one of America's greatest industrialists.

If you happen to drive a Chrysler vehicle today, you are driving one of the many descendents of the first car created by Walter Chrysler.

~

Commit your dreams to the Lord, and see what amazing things He will do.

It is God who works in you to will and to act according to his good purpose.

PHILIPPIANS 2:13

The end of all learning is to know God, and out of that knowledge to love and imitate Him.

Hunger for Knowledge

Joe proclaimed himself to be a perpetual student. His best friend often chided him, saying, "Joe, how can your brain hold all of those things you have learned?" The truth of the matter was that Joe had an insatiable hunger for knowledge. He made it a point to learn at least one thing every day. He was also a lifelong student of the Bible, believing it contained the wisdom of the ages. His children always said that he would have been a great diplomat because he could find something to talk about with virtually anyone.

As much as Joe was teased about being his family's wellspring of knowledge, if something significant happened in the world, Joe was the first person his family and friends turned to for perspective. The time he had spent

learning and acquiring knowledge inevitably brought with it a great measure of wisdom and understanding.

God created our minds with an infinite capacity to grow and a child-like curiosity to understand the "why" of things. Somewhere along the way, we quiet that curiosity and begin to think we've learned all we need to know. But there is joy in learning, and with the Internet at our fingertips, we can feed our curiosity and obtain answers to most of our questions.

So the next time you wonder about something, try plugging a key word into your Internet browser and see what interesting things you can learn. You, too, can be one people turn to when they need to know more.

~

Cultivate a love for learning.
Learn  something new every day.

Wisdom is supreme; therefore get wisdom.
Though is cost all you have, get understanding.
Esteem her, and she will exalt you;
embrace her, and she will honor you.

PROVERBS 4:7-8

You think me a child of my circumstances.

I make my circumstances.

Good Old-fashioned
Hard Work

When George Eastman was fourteen, his father died suddenly, leaving him and his mother nearly destitute. He left school to work full time to support himself and his mother resolving to make something of himself so that neither of them would ever have to be poor again. After working long days as a messenger boy, George would study accounting late into the night so that someday he might be able to better his position. Five years later, his tenacity paid off; he acquired a junior clerk position at a local bank. Finally, he could afford to dream.

George then became absorbed in photography, and before long, he put himself back on a rigorous schedule. After long days of work at the bank, in a makeshift laboratory he built in his mother's kitchen, George began to perform experiments late into the night. In the end, George successfully merged his passion for photography with his desire to succeed in business, resulting in the famed Eastman Kodak Company.

His success as an inventor and businessman came only in part due to his personal aspirations. His incredible dedication and diligent work ethic caused his dreams to be realized.

Like George Eastman, do you have aspirations beyond your current situation? Are you willing to pay the price to get there? As you set goals, commit them to God and diligently do your part. You can trust that God will reward your efforts and crown you with success.

~

Promotion comes to those
who dream big and work hard.

Lazy hands make a man poor,
but diligent hands bring wealth.

PROVERBS 10:4

Conscience is the root of all true courage;
if a man would be brave
let him obey his conscience.

Follow the Leader

After World War II, psychologists conducted a study to determine how people react to authority—whether or not they would perform unlawful or even atrocious acts if an authority figure were pressuring them to do so. Although they discovered that many caved in under the pressure, they also found that if just one person resisted and stood up for what was right, then exponentially higher numbers of people followed their lead.

In this day where situational ethics is touted, and the lines of right and wrong are not always as clearly discernable as they once were, the Bible stands in sharp contradiction. The Bible never changes. What was good and right when it was written is still good and right today. What was wrong then is still wrong. It is the absolute standard by which we are to order our lives.

It takes courage to stand up for what is right. Whether a person is a teenager resisting peer pressure to use drugs or an employee of a major corporation who is witness to unlawful accounting practices, we all face opportunities to take a stand. The higher the potential price for that stand, the more courage it takes to follow through.

Jesus knows exactly what we go through. His stand cost His life, but He did it for you and me. God will not leave you to take your stand alone. He promises to strengthen you and help you. Given the right circumstances, there may be many others who will follow your lead.

～

One courageous act inspires courage in others.

Do not fear, for I am with you;
do not be dismayed, for I am your God.
I will strengthen you and help you;
I will uphold you with my righteous
right hand.

Isaiah 41:10

133

When you make a mistake, don't look back
at it too long. Take the reason of the thing
into your mind, and then look forward.
Mistakes are lessons of wisdom. The past cannot
be changed. The future is yet in your power.

If at First You
Don't Succeed . . .

Guy was a successful independent contractor who enjoyed much respect in the community for his fair dealing and hard work. One year the National Forest Service announced a project to build a marina. No one bid on the project, and Guy decided that he could take it on. A friend at the bank cautioned him against taking the project, saying that a government contract would mire him in a bureaucratic runaround and ruin him. Convinced, however, that he could get the job done, Guy took on the project. Three years later, as his friend predicted, he was forced to liquidate all of his assets in order to pay his workers.

Guy, however, refused to let his mistake ruin him completely. Desperate to make money, Guy took any menial job he could and never stopped praying for God to show him how to make enough money to finish the marina. Finally, his wife told him, "Guy, why don't you stop telling God how to answer your prayers and tell Him instead that you are waiting to do His will, whatever it is."

Guy followed his wife's advice and began praying for God's will in his life. One week later, he awoke from an extraordinary dream. "I just had the strangest dream," he told his wife. "I dreamed that I had a big truck and I was vacuuming up prairie dogs!" Today Guy has one of the only licensed and most successful prairie-dog removal companies in the United States.

You're never finished unless you quit.

Forgetting what is behind and straining toward what is ahead, I press on toward the goal to win the prize for which God has called me heavenward in Christ Jesus.

PHILIPPIANS 3:13-14

A man there was, and they called him mad;
the more he gave, the more he had.

Givers Always Have Enough

Martha faced the daunting challenge of providing for her family throughout the Great Depression. "With my first child," she says, "the hard times had really just begun. By the time my third child was born, we were in the thick of the Depression." Martha recalls a day when all she and her two-year-old son had to eat for the whole day was one egg. "Of course I gave it to him," she says, "and I was pregnant at the time too." Another time, she recalls, "All we had to eat for the two weeks around Christmas was the leftover sandwiches that the Lutheran ladies brought over after their luncheons at the church.

"Although there was very little at the time," she attests, "we never went without, thanks to the generosity of others. All of us shared whatever we had." Now ninety-one, Martha says that she lives by something her father told her when she was a young woman: "God, cannot give to you unless you're giving to others." Now, living only on her retirement and social security, Martha says she's somehow able to give more to charity than she ever has in her life. "Giving heals and blesses us," she asserts. "Having known the generosity of others and having survived at times just because of it, I thank God that I now have the opportunity to give back." Pausing, she laughs, "I guess that's why He's kept me alive so long!"

~

God makes sure that a cheerful giver's well never runs dry.

"Give, and it will be given to you.
A good measure, pressed down,
shaken together and running over,
will be poured into your lap."

LUKE 6:38

In Christ we can move out of our
past into a meaningful present
and a breathtaking future.

God Creates Happy Endings

Ed grew up in an alcoholic home. His parents fought constantly. The only comfort he found was when he could leave his house or read his Bible. By the time he was an adult, he had built a protective wall around his emotions. He did attend church, however, and it was there that he met Deb and her four-year-old son, Johnny.

Deb's cocaine-addicted husband had abandoned her and Johnny when Johnny was only two. They had experienced a great deal of pain themselves, but there was a warmth about Deb that intrigued Ed. In contrast, Ed began to realize just how hardened he had become, and He asked God for help.

Over time Ed and Deb built a solid friendship, and the way Johnny's eyes lit up every time he saw Ed helped to soften the once-stony heart. Eventually, Ed and Deb married, and the three experienced a restoration that only God can bring.

Through all of their painful years, Ed and Deb never abandoned their commitment to God. Little did they know, in the midst of their pain, what blessings God had ahead for them.

Are you in the midst of your own painful situation? Jesus is a Friend who sticks closer than a brother. He is utterly trustworthy and will never abandon you. Because God is a good God, you can look up with confidence. He has good things in store for you.

Don't stop now. Good things are ahead!

Forget the former things;
Do not dwell on the past.
See, I am doing a new thing!
Now it springs up;
do you not perceive it?

Isaiah 43:18-19

139

What we think about when we are
free to think about what we will—
that is what we are or will soon become.

Whatcha Thinkin' 'Bout?

There is a popular saying, "You are what you eat." One could just as accurately say, "You are what you think." Proverbs 23:7 KJV puts it this way: "As a man thinketh in his heart, so is he." You don't like things the way they are? Try changing what you're thinking about.

It's no secret that if we dwell on our shortcomings, we could wind up depressed. Have past mistakes got you down? If we ask God to forgive us, He removes our sins so far away that He can't even remember them! If He's not thinking about them, why should we?

You can change. The Bible says you can be transformed, if you'll renew your mind to what God says about you. Find verses that tell you who you are in Christ, and begin filling your mind with those thoughts. You are a new creature in Christ; the old you died with Christ, the new you has emerged. You can do all things through Christ who strengthens you. God always causes you to triumph in Christ. Greater is He that is in you than he that is in the world.

There is a definite correlation between your input and your output: garbage in, garbage out. But the reverse is true as well: good things in, good things out. Begin today inputting good things about yourself. Like a tiny plant emerging from a seed, change is possible with God's help.

Having the same opinion of yourself
that God does will transform your life.

*Let God transform you into a new person
by changing the way you think.*

ROMANS 12:2 NLT

Four seasons fill the measure of the year;
There are four seasons in the mind of men.

What Season Are You In?

Like the natural seasons of spring, summer, fall, and winter, there are also seasons in our personal lives. What season are you in? If you are in the dead of winter, do not lose heart, for spring will surely come. But don't miss the unique blessings of winter. Few people realize that in winter, the plants are digging deep into the ground with their roots. Up top they look dead; but below, growth is taking place that will sustain them through the hot summer months. In the midst of this cold, dreary season, you may find your relationship with God will become more intimate than ever. Let your roots go deep into His love and His truth. Don't be discouraged by the cold. Spring is coming.

Or perhaps fall has come and you are reaping a harvest of blessings. Don't fool yourself into thinking it will always be like this, but do enjoy it. God will bring winter soon, and you will begin a time of growth once more.

One of the keys to living a full life is to recognize and appreciate the unique blessings that each season affords.

In whatever season you find yourself, the Creator of seasons is right there with you.

∾

Rejoicing in the Lord is appropriate in every season.

There is a time for everything,
and a season for every activity under heaven.

ECCLESIASTES 3:1

If we acknowledge God in all our ways,
he has promised safely to direct our steps, and in
our experience we shall find the promise fulfilled.

Hot or Cold?

Jill loved playing games with her preschooler, Cody. Besides, it was a nice distraction from the anxiety of knowing what to do next. Jill's husband, Jeff, had just completed his residency, and the couple had been seeking God as to where they were to settle down. Another consideration was whether to team up with another physician in an existing practice or to go out on his own. Jill had become anxious.

Meanwhile, Jill and little Cody played a game in which one of them hid an object and the other was to find it. The one who hid the item told the seeker whether they were hot or cold in relation to their proximity to the object.

"Getting warmer," Jill coaxed Cody. "Whoops, now you're getting cold. Warmer again, warmer, warmer, hot, hot, red hot!"

Cody's eyes sparkled as he looked into the flowerpot and found the special rock.

The game served as an object lesson for Jill. *"This is how I lead you,"* she sensed the Father saying. She realized that instead of trying to get the life plan for the next twenty years, she and Jeff should make one decision at a time. God would find a way to let them know if they were getting warmer or if they were heading in the wrong direction.

Are you trying to make important decisions? What is one baby step you can take? As you step out, be assured that God will lead you one step at a time.

~

God made you. He knows how to speak to you in a way that you can hear.

Whether you turn to the right or to the left, your ears will hear a voice behind you, saying, "This is the way; walk in it."

Isaiah 30:21

145

All the wealth in the world cannot be compared with the happiness of living together happily united.

After All Is Said and Done

Right after college, Liz went to work for a local hospice. Two of her first patients, Grace and Bob, taught her an invaluable life lesson. Grace was one of the most prestigious people Liz had ever met. She had earned her doctorate, served on the Council for the Arts, authored several books, and been the head of a university's arts and humanities department for years. Liz admired her for her many achievements. She noted, however, that although Grace's room was filled with flowers from well-meaning friends and colleagues, she had only the occasional visitor. Other than Liz being there, Grace died alone.

Bob, on the other hand, had been a schoolteacher. His room was the center of action, with a constant gaggle of grandchildren running around the room and a steady stream of visitors—

both family and friends. When Bob finally passed away, he did so peacefully, surrounded by those he loved.

These two individuals helped Liz decide what she wanted to do with her life. For her, the love of family and friends was more important than earning accolades. She did pursue higher education, but married and took a few years off to have a family. Although she did go on to develop her career, it was after her children were out of the nest. She always made sure that she put the relationships in her life before professional goals.

Where do you want to be at the end of your life? Are you on the right path?

When all is said and done, loving others and being loved is what life is all about.

How happy are those who fear the LORD—all who follow his ways! You will enjoy the fruit of your labor. How happy you will be! How rich your life! Your wife will be like a fruitful vine, flourishing within your home. And look at all those children! There they sit around your table as vigorous and healthy as young olive trees. That is the LORD's reward for those who fear him.

PSALM 128:1-4 NLT

What is a friend? A single soul
dwelling in two bodies.

Someone to Be Quiet With

It has been said that it isn't so much what you do that matters, but whom you do it with. Doing something with someone whose company you enjoy doubles the pleasure. Of course, we all need time to ourselves, time to unwind, but most activities are more enjoyable when doing them with a friend. It's fun to have someone to laugh with, and it creates happy memories.

A real friend is someone who enjoys the things you enjoy. Friends don't mind if the house is a wreck; they are there to see you. A real friend is someone with whom you can share your most intimate secrets without fear of being betrayed. A real friend is someone who loves you just as you are, even if you never change. A friend is someone you can cry with and rejoice with. Real friends are there when you need them.

There is another mark of really good friends—being able to be quiet with them. With people like this, you don't feel compelled to fill up airspace with meaningless chatter. You don't have to be talking to have a good time. There are those times when the two of you can't talk fast enough, wanting to share every minute detail. But it is a rare treasure to be able to just sit on the beach or travel in the car and just enjoy being together with a friend. Even in silence, two hearts can be knit together when those two people are friends.

Have you enjoyed the quiet with anyone lately?

~

Enjoying the quiet with someone can be as meaningful as sharing your whole heart.

A friend loves at all times.

PROVERBS 17:17

The sun makes ice melt;
Kindness causes misunderstanding,
mistrust, and hostility to evaporate.

Win 'em with Kindness

It was May's first job—outside of raising her family for twenty-some-odd years—and she was a bit nervous. She couldn't believe she had landed the position: lost-and-found clerk at the San Francisco Transit Lines. Betty, the front desk secretary, gave her a tour of the place, all the while dispensing bits of advice. After they had passed one office door, Betty warned, "You'd best steer clear of him. That's Charlie, and he's mean as a snake."

May, however, thought otherwise. *With the experience of raising four children and being married for twenty-five years,* thought May, *the one thing I've learned is you gotta win 'em with kindness.* May regarded Charlie as a challenge because he could be as mean and bitter as anyone she had ever met—just as Betty had warned. But May stuck to her guns and thought to herself, *There aren't many who are that hard and prickly on the outside who aren't marshmallows on the inside.*

Slowly but surely, May won over Charlie with her persistent kindness, and today she attests, "He became one of my truest and most enduring friends during the twenty years I was at the Transit." Though long since retired and living in another state, May still receives letters every Christmas from her dear friend, Charlie.

Kindness is the sunshine that
melts those who are cold as ice.

"Love your enemies! . . .
If you love only those who love you, what good is that?
Even corrupt tax collectors do that much."
MATTHEW 5:44-46 NLT

151

He is happiest, be he king or peasant,
who finds peace in his home.

Where Love Abides

Anthony Sweeney came to America from Ireland when he was seventeen years old. He married fellow Irish immigrant, Anna O'Connor. The two produced a family ten children strong. Anthony worked hard in the coal mines, and, although they had barely enough to get by, Anthony felt truly rich because of his family—a lovely wife, six beautiful daughters, and four strapping lads.

One evening Anthony returned home only to find his children in bitter strife with each other and their mother. Anthony said nothing and proceeded to get himself ready for supper. As they gathered around the table, the children grew silent, realizing that their father's sharp blue-eyed stare was upon them.

Finally, with stern ardency in his voice, he said, "We may not be that grand house on the hill. But that grand house is nothin' if there's no love in it!" The ten children sitting at the table didn't say another word. They learned something important that day, which they carried into their own families. No matter how many possessions one has or the size of the house, it's all worthless without love.

The house full of love is the richest house in the world.

Better a meal of vegetables where there is love,
than a fattened calf with hatred.

PROVERBS 15:17

He who is filled with love
is filled with God himself.

Never Too Late

Many call Mary a wonder. She's an energetic, effervescent ninety-year-old who embraces life each day with an undaunted positive attitude. She loves people, being with them and doing for them—which she does generously whenever she can. Every week, she takes out one of her grandchildren. Each time they say good-bye, she looks them in the eye and says, "I love you dearly."

Mary, however, will be the first one to tell you that she wasn't always like that. "Back when I was growing up," she says, "my parents were austere, serious people, and there wasn't a lot of affection." She then spent over thirty years in what she calls "an affectionless marriage." A widow, well into her fifties, Mary met her second husband, a man she describes as "the sweetest man that ever walked the earth. It took me time," she says, "but slowly I began to realize that the more love and affection I showed, the better I felt. So, even though I'm a wrinkled old lady, I guess it's not too late for me to let people know how much I love them."

～

It's never too late to love.

"A new command I give you:
Love one another. As I have loved you,
so you must love one another.
By this all men will know that
you are my disciples,
if you love one another."

JOHN 13:34-35

Seek the wisdom of the ages, but look
at the world through the eyes of a child.

If You Can't Say
Something Nice . . .

School was almost out for the summer, and the
Franklin family was planning a road trip to Florida.
With the children's end-of-the-year testing, field trips,
special projects, and ball games, the family needed a
break in the worst way. Their chaotic schedule kept everyone's nerves on edge, and the children were bickering
constantly. Even the parents, John and Christy, found
themselves nagging their children instead of calmly
setting and reinforcing boundaries.

"How on earth are we ever going to make that drive and
still enjoy the trip?" Christy questioned, contemplating
the twelve-hour drive that lay ahead.

It was then that Mimi, the children's grandmother, had
a stroke of genius "Tell you what, boys, I'm going to give
each of you fifteen dollars—"

"Fifteen dollars!" exclaimed six-year-old Jody.

Nine-year-old James was already dreaming of the souvenirs he could buy.

"Whoa, boys. Let me finish. I will give each of you fifteen dollars, but you can't spend it until the last day of your vacation. And there's a catch. Every time you argue, complain, or disobey, it will cost you a quarter, but whatever is left at the end of the week is yours to do with as you please."

No, neither boy got to keep the full fifteen dollars, but they didn't end up too badly. Jody had $12.50 and James $11.00, but more than anything else, the happy memories they made as a family were priceless.

Wisdom creates win/win situations.

Do everything without complaining or arguing, so that you may become blameless and pure, children of God without fault in a crooked and depraved generation, in which you shine like stars in the universe.

PHILIPPIANS 2:14-15

Man is never nearer the Divine
than in his compassionate moments.

The Face of Jesus

There was something about the woman's expressionless face and monotone voice that made Marcie wonder if there was more to the picture than met the eye. Marcie frequented the deli, and each time the scene was the same. The woman behind the counter looked like the walking dead. Finally, Marcie began to think that Divine intervention had brought this woman across her path, and she decided to take her on as a prayer project.

Every time Marcie saw her at the deli, she made it a point to always speak to the woman, calling her by the name on her nametag and making eye contact with her. It took several weeks before the woman acknowledged her, but eventually she even began to recognize Marcie and respond.

One day, Marcie decided to bring the woman a rose from her flower garden. The woman's eyes immediately teared up. Miraculously there was no one else at the deli at the time, and the woman began to open up. It turned out that a drunk driver killed her son the year before, and she was still grieving. She felt as if she had nothing to live for.

Marcie told the woman she had been praying for her and believed God had crossed their paths to show her the compassion of Jesus. It was the beginning of the woman's healing from her tragic ordeal, and eventually, she joined a grief recovery group. Because of one woman's sensitivity to the hurting heart of another, this grieving mother began to live again.

Stay sensitive. You may be the face of Jesus to someone with a hurting heart.

[Jesus] had compassion on them, because they were harassed and helpless, like sheep without a shepherd.

MATTHEW 9:35-37

Great works are performed,
not by strength,
but by perseverance.

The House that Persistence Built

There is a white colonial-style house in the middle of Black Forest, Colorado. As you make your way down the long driveway, you see that everything about the house is lovely. The ones who dwell there are just as lovely. They are hospitality personified, and their doors are always open.

The house is a miracle of sorts and was built against all odds. It stands as a monument to the man who built it out of love for his family. After buying the five-acre parcel of land, the man spent every evening after a full day's work and every weekend for a year building the house. The fact that it was one of the worst winters on record for the area would have deterred most, but this sturdy soul pressed on. Once almost breaking his hand with the hammer and another time falling off the roof, this determined husband and father worked in the dark and through all seasons, whatever it took. Despite exhaustion and long and lonely hours, the man faithfully resisted the temptation to quit, unswerving from his goal.

Finally the man's perseverance paid off as he presented his labor of love to his family. You could call it the "House that Persistence Built." And to this day, it continues to be a blessing to all who are fortunate enough to pass through its doors.

~

Perseverance keeps the goal in
sight and never, never quits.

*Do not throw away your confidence; it will
be richly rewarded. You need to persevere.*

HEBREWS 10:35-36

Let temporal things serve thy use, but
the eternal be the object of thy desire.

The Art of Distraction

We are bombarded daily by a constant barrage of audio and visual messages, information, and stimuli. Whether we are driving in our cars, standing in the grocery store checkout line, or sitting at home watching television, we continually receive messages telling us that we *have to have* a certain thing or we should look a certain way. It is easy to fall into the trap and allow "them" to dictate what you need in order to be happy. The sad thing is, when people work so hard to get what it is that they *just have* to have, they find it only satisfies for a moment—until the next commercial touts something even better.

It is the job of advertisers to distract us. They know that if they keep us looking at something long enough, we will begin to desire it. The bottom line is that they are after your billfold, and they'll fight to get at it any way they can.

But we don't have to fall for the trap! Jesus came to give us abundant life, a life that will satisfy the craving of our souls. The apostle Paul told us that the way to develop this inner life of peace is to think on the things of the Spirit. The more you think on spiritual things, the more you will desire them in your heart.

Allow yourself to get "distracted" by the Bible. Decide you are going to open it instead of flipping through a magazine, and just see what happens.

~

Feeding your desire for spiritual things will result in a desire for more.

Those who live in accordance with the Spirit have their minds set on what the Spirit desires. . . . The mind controlled by the Spirit is life and peace.

ROMANS 8:5-6

As long as you live,
keep learning how to live.

Unexpected Education

Donna graduated at the top of her class from Columbia University, worked as an accountant for six years, and raised four children. She thought she had pretty much been through and seen it all, and she looked forward to a stress-free, relaxing retirement.

Donna's youngest daughter, April, was pregnant with her first baby. Donna was thrilled because it meant she would be a grandmother. When the baby finally arrived, however, all were shocked to discover that the baby was born with Down's syndrome. Donna was at a loss as to how to comfort her daughter and offer her support. She was even more shocked when she saw how beautifully April handled the family's awkward confusion. She simply beamed with joy as

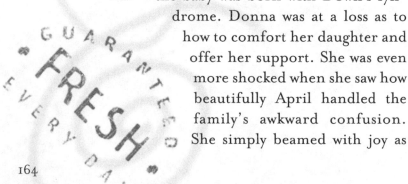

she held her little Michael, showing everyone that he was the most perfect gift that God could have given her.

With April working part-time, Donna had her opportunity to help out by keeping Michael. Those who knew Donna before Michael attest that this one little child has had a greater effect on her than anything else she has ever encountered. "A lot of my expectations and standards have changed," she says, "and I now realize how little I knew about life, the complexity and beauty of it, before I had the privilege of knowing Michael."

Life often throws us an unexpected curve ball, but it isn't the end of the world. Reach out to God for His grace, and let Him show you the hidden blessings.

Whatever you are going through,
seek the lesson that can be learned.

The heart of the discerning acquires knowledge;
the ears of the wise seek it out.

PROVERBS 18:15

We make a living by what we get,
but we make a life by what we give.

Recognize Your Gift

Lori enjoyed her job as a senior sales consultant, but after some soul-searching, she realized that she wasn't contributing anything back to the world. Worse yet, she didn't think she had anything special to offer.

Her mother knew otherwise. "You have plenty of gifts and talents! You are one of the most generous and caring people I know, and you'd do anything for anyone. You enjoy making people happy. And don't forget, you have real gift with animals."

Lori knew that what her mother said was true, but she didn't know how to put those qualities to work for others. Her best friend, Gail, was a nurse at the Hospice Care Center, and she had an idea. "We have several volunteers who visit the center, offering their unique talents to bless the patients. I think you should call our volunteer coordinator to see if you can't work out something with your dogs."

Bringing her dogs to visit the patients who liked animals was a great success. Before she knew it, Lori found herself at the helm of the new hospice pet therapy program, which turned out to be one of the most popular with the patients.

What gifts do you possess? If you're having difficulty discerning them, ask someone you trust who knows you well. Then offer those gifts to God and ask Him to give you creative ideas to put them to work. He designed you, and He knows just the spot where you can make the greatest impact.

~

You have a Divine destiny.
Use your gifts for God's glory!

Just as each of us has one body with many members, and these members do not all have the same function, so in Christ we who are many form one body, and each member belongs to all the others. We have different gifts, according to the grace given us.

ROMANS 12:4-6

Integrity is the noblest possession.

A Man of His Word

Jim had been out of work for nearly a year. Even though he eventually found a job, he and his wife felt like they just couldn't catch up financially. Then their hot water heater died. During the past year they had received so much help from family and friends that they couldn't even think of asking any of them to help again. Finally, he wrote his father a letter, asking if he could lend him the money for the hot water heater. He assured his father that he would pay back the loan as soon as he was able. His father sent a check, no questions asked, and never brought up the subject again.

It took Jim and his wife a few years to get back on their feet again. They had been forced to rely on credit cards for their bare necessities, but now, five years later, all of their debts were finally paid off. Jim wrote his father a letter thanking him for his generous loan and enclosed a check for the amount plus fifteen percent interest for the five years. One month later, Jim received the last letter he would ever receive from his father. The envelope contained the check that Jim had sent to his father and a very short note that said, "I am really impressed with your integrity and loyalty, son. That is more than enough repayment for me."

~

God keeps His Word, and He blesses those who keep theirs.

In my integrity you uphold me
and set me in your presence forever.

PSALM 41:12

In his love he clothes us, enfolds us
and embraces us; that tender love
completely surrounds us, never to leave us.

A Glimpse into God's Love

The miracle of the tiny being growing within Anna changed the way she looked at herself and the world around her. It was simply amazing to her that the Creator allowed her and her husband to create the precious child in her womb.

She was aware that even as she felt so much love for a little being that she had never seen, how much more must God love us! She began to comprehend God's love in a way that she never had before. In the Bible, God compares His love to that of a mother hen. "I have longed to gather your children together, as a hen gathers her chicks under her wings" (Matthew 23:37). The tender love a mother feels toward her young comes straight from the heart of God.

It has been said that the intense nurturing and protective love a mother has for her children is the earthly love that comes closest to the love the Father has for us. The apostle Paul prayed that we would grasp the length, the breadth, the height, and the depth of that love, assuring us that absolutely *nothing* can ever separate us from it.

Perhaps that is why God allows us to participate in the whole birthing and parenting process. Even though we will never fully comprehend it, every time we experience love for our children, it serves as a reminder of the fathomless love the Father has for us.

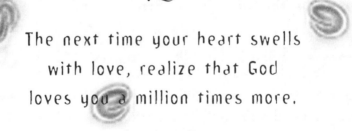

The next time your heart swells
with love, realize that God
loves you a million times more.

As a mother comforts her child,
so will I comfort you.

ISAIAH 66:13

As prayer is the voice of man to God,
so revelation is the voice of God to man.

Eyes to See

Have you ever looked for your sunglasses only to find them sitting right on top of your head? Have you ever roamed the house looking for your car keys only to discover that they were in your hand the whole time?

Moses of the Old Testament could have related. When God called him to lead the Hebrew people out of Egypt, Moses was looking for a way to convince them that he was God's chosen leader. God then asked Moses what he had in his hand. "A staff," Moses replied. Time and time again, Moses used that simple staff and wrought wonders. He struck a rock with it, and water gushed out. He touched the Nile River with it, and the water turned to blood. Perhaps the most memorable of all was when he touched the waters of the Red Sea, and they parted so the Israelites could escape their enemies.

The point of these examples is to illustrate that often the very thing we are looking for is right in front of us, but we need eyes to see it. Have you been praying for God to use you? Ask Him to reveal what you already have that you can use to bless others. Or are you seeking an answer to your prayer? You might already have the answer but haven't recognized it as such. Whatever the circumstances, God has answers for you. Ask Him to give you eyes to see, then keep your eyes peeled.

Seeing through God's eyes
brings everything into focus.

Open my eyes that I may see
wonderful things in your law.
PROVERBS 119:17-19

Do not let the good things in
life rob you of the best things.

Keeping the Main Thing
the Main Thing

Anyone who knew Virginia described her as someone who had her act together. And generally speaking, she saw herself in much the same way—until she had children.

When Virginia's first child was born, she went through a crisis of sorts. All of a sudden, instead of ending each day with all of her to-do's checked off her list, she was lucky if she achieved even a couple of her objectives. The entire universe seemed to revolve around her baby, and anyone who has children can attest to the fact that it does. Virginia loved being a mother, but was constantly frustrated that she wasn't able to be as "together" as she once had been. There were phone calls to be returned, laundry to be done, and a whole family of dust bunnies to be cleared from the corners of her home.

Her mother helped her gain perspective. Virginia came to realize that what she was feeling was normal, but that she was going to have to become much more flexible. Taking care of her baby obviously came first. Everything else had to take a number. Instead of trying to conquer everything on her list each day, she began to choose one or two of the most important tasks. The other things had to wait—and that was OK.

It took practice and a lot of letting go of previous expectations, but Virginia became much more flexible and was able to enjoy motherhood to its fullest.

~

It's important to be flexible
if you don't want to break.

"There is really only one thing worth being concerned about. Mary has discovered it."

Luke 10:42 NLT

If you treat an individual as he is, he will stay
as he is; but if you treat him as if he were
what he ought to be and could be, he will become
what he ought to be and what he could be.

A Wise Solution

When George first joined the army, he experienced problems with things disappearing from his locker. Most of the guys knew that his locker could be jimmied open easily, so George thought any number of his comrades could have done it. At first only small things disappeared: fingernail clippers, a picture, his metal comb. One night George meticulously polished his belt buckle and placed it in his locker. When he went to retrieve it the next morning, he found a very green, tarnished belt buckle in its place. Then George noticed Jake Burns, a scrawny new recruit, wearing a bright shiny belt buckle, which George was fairly certain was his.

Instead of confronting him, which would have embarrassed Jake and put him on the defensive, George decided to try another approach. He struck up a conversation with Jake and said, "Hey, Burns, I've got a problem. Someone's been stealing stuff out of my locker. I noticed that you're in here more than I am, so I was wondering if you would keep an eye on my stuff. See if you can't figure out who's been doing it." Burns agreed and, according to George, nothing ever was missing from his locker again.

Seek the wise solution so that everybody wins.

"Be wise as serpents and harmless as doves."
MATTHEW 10:16 NKJV

I will place within them as a guide
my umpire Conscience,
whom if they will hear,
Light after light well used they shall attain,
And to the end persisting, safe arrive.

God Will Guide You

When Ellie was sixteen, she approached her parents about becoming an exchange student. Her parents calmly replied that if it was something that she really wanted to do, she needed to research the information and investigate scholarship opportunities, because they could not afford to send her.

After taking all the necessary steps, an exchange organization accepted her into the program, and she even received a full-tuition scholarship. When her departure date was about two months away, however, she began to get anxious. What was she doing? Why was she tearing herself away from the familiar and abandoning her comfort zone? She discussed the situation with her parents.

The three prayed about the situation and asked God to confirm His will, one way or the other. After praying, her parents encouraged her to isolate her fear and determine what was in her heart. After some quiet time with God, Ellie could see that her fear was based more on the unknown aspects of the trip and not necessarily on the trip itself. In her heart, she felt that she was indeed to take the trip, and her parents, also at peace, supported her decision.

From that point on, Ellie's excitement returned. The trip turned out to be one of the most memorable and life-impacting experiences of her life. During her trip, Ellie received the call to serve as a full-time missionary, which she did, after graduating from college.

~

God's peace is our most reliable guide.

Let the peace . . . from Christ rule (act as umpire continually)
in your hearts [deciding and settling with finality]
all questions that arise in your minds].

COLOSSIANS 3:15 AMP

Faith is to believe what you
do not yet see; the reward for this
faith is to see what you believe.

Against All Odds

Guidance counselor Chuck Banes had great hopes for Jennifer. She was by no means the student voted most likely to succeed. On the contrary, she would have been voted most likely to drop out. Numerous times, Jennifer ended up in Chuck's office, sent by the principal as an alternative to expulsion. Each time Chuck would tell Jennifer, "You are smart. I see in you the potential to succeed, and I know that one day you will." He couldn't put his finger on it, but somehow, despite her circumstances, he knew that she would defy the odds and pull herself out of the rut she was in.

Before graduation, Jennifer was expelled for drug use. Chuck lost track of her completely, but he continued to pray for her. Six years later, there was a knock at his door. When he answered, Chuck saw a face he would never forget. It was Jennifer, but she looked like a completely different person. She had enrolled in night school, received her GED, started studying at a community college, and recently had been accepted into a university on an ROTC scholarship.

The year after she was expelled, she ran away from home. "I had a lot of time to think," she said, "and I decided that I wanted to prove all those teachers wrong who thought that I wouldn't amount to anything. But even more, I wanted to prove you right."

The love of God in you can inspire others to greatness.

Love . . . is ever ready to believe the best of every person, its hopes are fadeless under all circumstances. . . . Love never fails.

1 CORINTHIANS 13:7-8 AMP

Each of us will have our own different ways
of expressing love and care for the family.
But unless that is a high priority,
we will find that we may gain the
whole world and lose our own children.

First Things First

Dave and Cindy were married while Dave was in medical school. Cindy was wonderfully supportive throughout all his doctoral studies and residency, fully understanding the commitment she had made. Eventually, Dave's career soared. He became the head oncologist at the hospital and was a regular speaker on the lecture tour. He even spent a summer in Cambridge doing research. Through it all Cindy was faithfully supportive and bore him two children.

At the end of the summer at Cambridge, Dave returned home from work one evening to find his three-year-old son

GUARANTEED
FRESH
EVERY DAY

playing in the yard. On seeing his father, Jack ran crying into the house. It was a startling revelation that his precious son wasn't comfortable enough to allow his own father to pick him up. Dave's long absences had taken their toll. Even Cindy's patience was wearing thin.

But the story doesn't end there. Together he and Cindy reevaluated their priorities and made changes. He no longer spent extended periods away from his family. He limited his lecture engagements, taking his family with him when possible. He also limited his hours at the hospital. Dave also made it a point to take one of his children on a "date" each week to stay connected to them. He and Cindy scheduled regular times together and an occasional weekend away. Dave was fortunate because he was able to turn his ship around before it was too late.

Do your priorities need rearranging?

God's plan for success won't cost you your family.

"No one can serve two masters; for either he will hate the one and love the other, or he will hold to one and despise the other."

MATTHEW 6:24 NASB

Anxiety is the interest paid
on trouble before it's due.

Enjoy the Moment

Carrie was a champion worrier. Most of her anxieties were about things that might or might not happen in the future. She was so busy living in the "what ifs" of the future that she was being robbed of the joy of today.

One day while she was reading her Bible, the words practically jumped off the page at her: "Cast all your anxiety on him because he cares for you," (1 Peter 5:7). She had read this verse many times before, but the words "he cares for you" somehow suddenly came alive. She had a fresh revelation that she could let go of her worries, because God cared for *her*. She could trust Him to take care of her "what ifs."

From that point on, Carrie became more aware of her anxious thoughts and made a concerted effort to cast them on the Lord immediately. She pictured herself actually hurling her worries to Him.

She also made a real effort to live in the present. If she caught herself thinking about the future, she'd stop and make herself think in the here and now. It took practice, but slowly she began to change the way she thought. As a result, she began experiencing a peace that she hadn't even known existed.

What kinds of things do you think about? Do they bring you peace or cause you worry? If you find yourself worrying, try doing what Carrie did and see if you don't start enjoying life more.

~

Living in the here and now and enjoying each moment is a gift you give yourself.

Cast your cares on the LORD
and he will sustain you;
he will never let the righteous fall.

PSALM 55:22

Sometimes it's a form of love just to talk to somebody with whom you have nothing in common and still be fascinated by their presence.

Seeing through God's Eyes

While spending a year studying at a university in Lyon, France, Sean ran into many misconceptions about America and Americans. "This surprised me," he said, "because I expected the French to be more educated about their opinions—which is, I guess, a misconception of mine about the French!"

When one of his newfound friends discovered that Sean was from Texas, his friend told him that he thought all Texans were cowboys. Others thought that all Americans lived in big cities, and that murders, muggings, and robberies were a part of every American's daily life. "It's understandable," Sean says, "that since most movies are American-made, many people around the world believe that what they see on the silver screen is what we are actually like."

It is human nature to accept stereotypes as reality, when so often they are not accurate. It's easier to judge by what we see with our eyes than to take the time to know and understand what is beneath the surface.

As believers we are to view people as simply that: precious people for whom Jesus gave His life. Regardless of the car they drive, the part of town they live in, their skin color, their educational background, or any other characteristics, all people are treasures to God, made in His image.

If you catch yourself thinking stereotypically, take a look through the eyes of God. Chances are, you'll like what you see!

~

**People don't belong in boxes.
They are part of God's dream.**

*Accept each other just as Christ
has accepted you; then God
will be glorified.*

ROMANS 15:7 NLT

187

There is not enough darkness, in all the world,
to put out the light of even one small candle.

Be a Hero

We all love heroes—people who go against the grain to stand up for what is right, regardless of the cost. They are people of principle, and we admire them because they are so rare. When it comes to us personally, we know just how hard it is to stand alone, especially in the face of others pressuring us to go with the flow of the world.

But isn't that part of the life of a believer? Jesus said that we would be in the world but not of the world. The apostle Paul exhorted us to come out from the world and be separate. In another place the Bible says that we are peculiar people, a royal priesthood. Yet another passage describes us as strangers and foreigners during our tenure on earth.

There is a very good reason we are to go against the grain—

the world that tries to squeeze us into its mold is itself engulfed in darkness. How will they see if we hide our lights under a bushel? Paul said that we "shine like stars in the universe" as we hold out the word of life. (See Philippians 2:15.) The world needs what we have.

No one ever said that the life of a believer would be easy, but we have a Savior who loves us and promises to help us. He gives us the grace we need to take a bold stand when necessary, and like our Savior, we can be the light of the world.

Be a hero. Let your light shine!

The people walking in darkness
have seen a great light;
on those living in the land of the shadow of death
a light has dawned.

ISAIAH 9:2

Acknowledgments

Alexander Maclaren (6), Abraham Lincoln (8), John Donne (10), Ralph Waldo Emerson (12,130), François Duc de La Rochefoucauld (14), Author Unknown (16,50,58,66,92,96,110,120), Sir Thomas Browne (18), John Baillie (20), French Proverb (22), Blaise Pascal (24), Danish Proverb (26), Frances J. Roberts (28), Letitia Elizabeth Landon (30), Marcus Tillius Cicero (32), John Powell (34), John Bunyan (36,136), Mary Carolyn Davies (38), Thomas Huxley (40), Vance Havner (42), Edwin Markham (44), Henry Wadsworth Longfellow (46), Reinhold Niebuhr (48), J.M. Usteri (52), Charles Wesley (54), C.S. Lewis (56), Horace Bushnell (60), William Shakespeare (62,112), John Oxenham (64), Martin Luther (68), Sydney J. Harris (70), Matthew Henry (72), Oswald Chambers (74), Robert Harold Schuller (76), Ann Landers (78), German Proverb (80), Bessie Anderson Stanley (82), Nathaniel Hawthorne (84), Colin Urquhart (86), Sir Thomas Browne (88), Charles Dudley Warner (90), Richard C. Woodsome (94), David Hume (98), Tryon Edwards (100), Angelus Silesius (102), Jean Baptiste Poqueli Molière (104), Ralph E. Hudson (106), Samuel Dickey Gordon (108), Thomas Jefferson (114), Horace (116), George Seaton Bowes (118), John R. Mott (122), Saint Bernard of Clairvaux (124), Catherine Wood Marshall (126), John Milton (128,178), J.F. Clarke (132), Hugh White (134), Erwin W. Lutzer (138), A.W. Tozer (140), John Keats (142), Edward Payson (144), Margaret of Youville (146), Aristotle (148), Albert Schweitzer (150), Johann Wolfgang von Goethe (152,176), Saint Augustine of Hippo (154,180), Ron Wild (156), Joseph H. Hertz (158), Samuel Johnson (160), Thomas à Kempis (162), Alexis de Toqueville (164), Sir Winston Churchill (166), Latin Proverb (168), Julian of Norwich (170), John Henry Newman (172), Buster Rothman (174), Michael Green (182), William Ralph Inge (184), David Byrne (186), Robert Atkin (188).

Also available:
Coffee Break Devotions: Cappuccino

If you have enjoyed this book,
or if it has impacted your life,
we would like to hear from you.

Please contact us at:

Honor Books
An Imprint of Cooks Communications Ministries
4050 Lee Vance View
Colorado Springs, CO 80918

Or by e-mail at *www.cookministries.com*